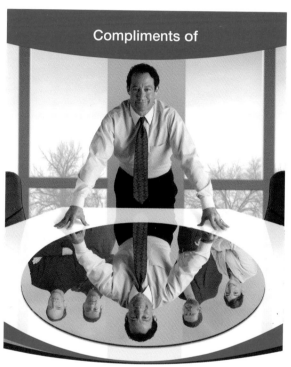

Compliments of

TEC. CHIEF EXECUTIVES WORKING TOGETHER | better leaders **decisions** results

THE WORLD'S LEADING CHIEF EXECUTIVE ORGANIZATION

WWW.TEC-CANADA.COM

Fog Lights

*Piercing the Fog of
Everyday Business*

P. Bruce Hunter

Library and Archives Canada In Publication
Hunter, P. Bruce 1954 -
        Fog Lights: Piercing The Fog Of Everyday Business
        P. Bruce Hunter
1. Small Business - Management 2. Leadership 3. Customer Relations I. Title
HD62.7.H96 2008   658.02'2   c2008-901835-4

ISBN: 978-0-9809073-0-8

Published by Lighthouse 360
3 Deepwood Crescent
Don Mills, Ontario
M3C 1N7

To Peg,
my wife and best friend.

And to Kelly and Stacey,
with love and great pride.

Table Of Contents

Part Three — Leadership Fog Lights

Appendices

Acknowledgments

The process of writing this book has been a journey: a journey of self-discovery and of learning from and about those around me. One of the most important things this process has taught me is that virtually everyone has a keen desire to be of assistance. People are good.

It is always difficult to select just a few people to thank in such a limited space. Like an iceberg, for the 10 percent I recognize who are "above the surface," there were 90 percent more "beneath the surface" whose contributions must go unremarked upon, but are in no way unappreciated. Of those who figured prominently in helping craft my thoughts and words, my thanks go out to:

First, my family. I owe a debt of gratitude to all my immediate family for listening to a relentless stream of stories from and about the book. Thanks especially to my wife Peg, who steadfastly encouraged me in this quest and endured no end of discussion about both subject and content. Without her support, it wouldn't have happened. Thanks to my daughters, Kelly and Stacey, who listened politely to each "eureka" moment even when the subject matter didn't quite measure up to "Much Music." Thanks also to my brother Tom, who provided much needed remedial grammar lessons and my sister Susan, who never tired of listening and providing excellent input along the way.

This book has become almost legendary even in the extended Hunter household, becoming a fixture of discussion at nearly every family get-together. Tom's wife Barb and their two daughters Christine and Laura, as well as Susan's husband Peter and their kids, John, Jennifer, Katie and Andrew, all contributed to the discussions. The influence of all of this collective input helped create the canvas upon which many of these thoughts and ideas are drawn. Thanks also of course to my mother, Moira, whose ongoing interest and commentary made so many early mornings so much more bearable. Thanks to the Buckingham clan in St. John's, Newfoundland — a very special group, particularly Peg's mother Alice, who spent hours chatting with me on her too infrequent trips to Toronto or in her kitchen in St. John's while the rest of the house was asleep.

Second, friends — new and old. Jim Barnes and I have shared an extraordinary journey together. It began when I was a student in the mid-70s at Queen's University in Kingston, and Jim was a professor on sabbatical from Memorial. I honestly can't remember which marketing course of his I took, only that I enjoyed it tremendously. In one of those strange twists in life, he and I met again over two decades later at Kraft Canada. In working and sharing ideas with Jim, I discovered that there was always one constant: he inspires. Always accommodating and never judgmental, my chats with him still give me tremendous intellectual stimulation and inspiration. Jim has graciously allowed me to comment on his creative endeavors as well as providing much needed commentary on my work (he shares top spot in the grammar department with my brother Tom). I truly appreciate his friendship and support.

Duncan McGregor also occupies a special place of friendship. While he and I share many of the same values, even a saint would have a tough time measuring up to Duncan. I greatly appreciate his steadfast, genuine interest in both my content and the process of writing. He also provided me his own "advice list," learned through many years of business leadership. Thanks for being a true friend and counselor — and for your indirect financial support through your golf bets with me on the links! I should also make special mention of Yong Quek and Peter and Marie-Paul Gallop for their "on course" conversation and advice.

Inspiration to break through the inertia of writing often came from Michael Hepworth. I've come to know Michael a little more recently than some of the others mentioned previously, but we've shared long chats about marketing and business and exchanged moments of penetrating brilliance (to us, anyway). It was at one such meeting that Michael leaned over and handed me his finished book, *The Streetsmart Marketer*. More than anything else, this provided me the impetus for driving through to the finish line on my own book. Thanks, Michael, for getting me off my butt.

Marc Schwarz is my editor and ghost-writer. Marc and I have never actually met, he living in Austin, Texas and me in Toronto. We met "virtually" through a circuitous route of other individuals, and we have spoken at least once a week for the past year. Marc is a savant. There are few individuals I've met who have as broad a knowledge base, who are as brilliant in the turn of a phrase and who can stand listening to me extolling some grand new theory or idea for sometimes hours on end. I owe much to Marc. In a relatively short period of time, and despite the distance, I consider him a friend and trusted advisor.

The alumni from BBDO, the advertising agency with which I worked as a partner while at Kraft, also figured prominently in the creation of this book. My former account director, Daryl Aitken, and I spent many hours discussing and debating various marketing and business schemes. Bob Hawton, BBDO's former creative director and later a business partner at Kraft, labored intensely in reading, proofing and editing a number of iterations of my earlier attempts at the creative process. Thank you!

Some people are intertwined in our lives. For me, one such person is my long-time friend Ian Bell, whom I met at age 16 while we were both serving as counselors-in-training at summer camp. Later we were roommates at university, worked on oil rigs together and now, almost 30 year later, serve together as "Chairs" in an organization known as TEC ("The Executive Committee"). Through it all, Ian has been an intermittent but important participant, confidant and counselor. Ian, thanks for your help — not just with this latest effort of mine, but through the years. Thank you as well to Peter Reid, another such friend whom I first met at that same summer camp. He too has been a stalwart supporter of mine through the years.

Thanks also to all the people in my Don Mills neighborhood who have taken an interest in this project: (in no particular order) Anne and David MacPhee, Doris and Paul Bies, Linda and Richard Jussaume, and Maureen and Frank Rooke. Many of the ideas in this book were honed on long walks with the dogs, cottage visits and weekend BBQs. I'm indebted to you all and those others in the community who were supportive.

I also owe much to the Fosters: Jane, Stephen, Christy, Paul and Mark. Those long chats on the beach at the cottage helped immensely in the writing of the book (as did the jokes via the net, Jane).

I would be remiss if I left out Jim Caverhill, a long-time friend and supporter. Our paths may not cross as frequently today as they once did, but I felt your presence throughout the process.

Third, my business friends. In the six years since leaving the hallowed halls of Corporate America, I've met some of the most fascinating and engaging people, beginning with Brian Vallis and his company, 180 Solutions. You helped me rid myself of a lot of my corporate baggage and come to understand the trials and tribulations of the SME owner. Thanks to my friends at TEC, who helped me become a more effective advisor through our meetings both in camera and outside. I owe also, a great debt to the folks at Marshall Fenn who drove the creative process in designing the cover, layout and providing much needed "thought buddy" time. It started with Jim Kabrajee and extended through his team to James, Steven and Laura.

Thanks to my friends at Kraft, both here in Canada and in the States. You'll always hold a special place in my heart, as will those folks from General Foods (which no longer exists) who have kept in touch over the years. John Cassaday and Paul Robertson top that list, but there are many, many more to whom I am indebted.

A final thanks to all who helped but have not been singled out for special note. I have greatly appreciated your support and counsel.

Introduction

In the movie *Forrest Gump*, Tom Hank's character Forrest was moved to start running one day following the sudden departure of his life-long love, Jenny. He begins to jog, first to the end of the road, then to the end of town, eventually to the end of the country. After three years, two months, fourteen days and sixteen hours, followed now by a sizable crowd eager to see the end of his epic journey, Forrest just. . . stops.

The puzzled crowd falls silent, waiting for him to utter some profound statement, some explanation, some revelation. He pauses, then says simply: "I'm pretty tired. I think I'll go home now."

That's often how I feel after trudging through one more business book that promises how its "big idea" will transform my outlook, my business, my life or my professional relationships. Hundreds of pages later, no more enlightened than when I started, all I feel is pretty tired.

Thirty years in business has taught me that rarely does one big idea make the difference between success and failure. Sure, there are genuine eureka moments, but let's face it, they're few and far between. The devil, as they say, is in the details. What I needed in my leadership roles — and what my small and medium enterprise (SME) clients need — are multiple techniques for dispelling the fog that seems to surround so much of what we do in business, making us indecisive, unsure, mistake-prone, fearful and primed for failure.

That's the basis for *Fog Lights: Piercing the Fog of Everyday Business* — practical, easy-to-implement insights designed to pierce that fog and make your path to business growth more visible. Some are somewhat unconventional, others just good sense. All have been time-tested and field-proven. You'll find advice you can immediately put to productive use in a variety of areas critical for business success. Each of these "fog lights" is accompanied by specific keys to action to help you painlessly and efficiently execute the principles you've just read.

Fog Lights is built on a foundation of five bedrock themes, all of which have been essential to success for both me and my clients:

- **Applying an outside-in perspective to your business.** That means learning to see through the eyes of your customers and other external stakeholders. There's no shortage of literature on this subject by self proclaimed customer service gurus, but the fact is that most companies preach it far better than they practice it.

- **The importance of "planning in reverse."** Not only is it key, as Stephen Covey said, "to start with the end in mind," you must also map out your path from the end to the beginning. I've found from experience that this is critical to gain the traction necessary to achieve your goals.

- **The role of inclusion.** Please note that I do not use the word "empower." This is not touchy-feely stuff: no group hugs, no abdication of leadership in favor of some sort of cozy consensus. No, this is about leveraging the power of many to align focus, not disperse it. Inclusive policies harness your employees' talents, ideas and abilities; instructive policies simply dictate what is expected with little regard for context or input. Growth depends on the former.

- **The need to focus and simplify.** More often ends up actually being less. Strong businesses have one-track minds. Relentless in the pursuit of their core concept enables them to differentiate themselves and become successful.

- **Why you should adhere to "timeless values."** The essence of good business practice and personal conduct has remained unchanged since man first traded animal skins for grain. Proven values — honesty, trust, respect for others, hard work — will always trump fads based on quick wins or ill-gotten gains.

The ideas and suggested actions contained in this book have consistently helped me, my colleagues and my clients clear a path through the fog of everyday business life. If you turn them on, I'm convinced these Fog Lights will be of considerable value to you as well.

PART ONE

Customer Fog Lights

*"If you listen closely enough,
your customers will explain your business to you."*

— Peter Shutz, TEC Speaker

The Copernican Shift
Successful companies revolve around their customers

For nearly two millennia, mankind had believed that it was the center of the universe, that the Earth was the fixed point around which everything else in the cosmos revolved. A few brave voices — the ancient Greek astronomer Aristarchus among them — dissented, claiming that the sun was the true axis of the solar system, but they were shouted down as heretics or dismissed as fools.

And so it remained until 1543, when Nicolas Copernicus caused shockwaves with his magnum opus, *On the Revolutions of the Celestial Spheres*. In it, Copernicus argued persuasively for a heliocentric model. The sun, not the earth, was the true center of the known universe.

Copernicus had dangled his theory decades earlier in a short, handwritten book he called the *Little Commentary*, but knowing the kind of reaction (and persecution) that might result from a more detailed treatment of this sensitive subject, he delayed publishing a more comprehensive version until the year he died. In fact, legend has it that when the first printed copy of *Revolutions* was placed in his hands, he awoke from a stroke-induced coma, looked at the result of his life's work, and died peacefully.

The philosophical firestorm ignited by Copernicus did not die with him. In years that followed, adherents and opponents of what came to be known as the Copernican System fought each other in print and in court. The cost was sometimes frighteningly high — the Italian cosmologist and philosopher Giordano Bruno was burned at the stake for (in part) his support of Copernicus' theories.

Even as eminent a figure as Galileo was tried by the Inquisition and forced by threat of imprisonment, torture or worse to recant his belief that it was the Earth and not the sun that moved. "Epur si muovo," he is alleged to have whispered after his official statement. *"And yet it does move!"*

Copernicus' worldview, it seems, would still have the last word.

US VS. THEM

I was recently invited to speak to a marketing group for a biotech company that manufactures pharmaceutical products for people diagnosed with a severe, debilitating disease. Following my talk on strategy development, the audience broke into several groups to build a "SWOT" analysis: a summary of the company's strengths, weaknesses, opportunities and threats.

As I listened to the exercise, I sat dumbfounded at the lack of empathy the participants had toward their direct and indirect "customers," the doctors and patients who used their products. The whole discussion focused solely on the challenges that this particular company was facing; at no time during the meeting did any of the assembled marketing execs make even a single comment that considered the customers' point of view, the customers' perceptions, the customers' needs. "Us" was their real concern, not "them."

For all the industry talk these days about being customer-centric, most companies live in a pre-Copernican state of mind: they expect their customers to revolve around their offerings instead of adjusting their offerings to revolve around the customers' needs and expectations.

After about 30 minutes of watching the SWOT exercise at the biotech company, I stopped the activity to ask a few questions. "What issues do you think the doctor is dealing with when doing a consult with a patient? Is there a way you could help him or her? What are they feeling? What about the patient attending the consult? How do they feel? What could you do for them?"

The room went silent. Not a paper stirred.

It was pretty evident that none of these people had ever, to borrow a phrase coined by my friend, author and professor, Dr. James Barnes, "put on their customer hat." They were used to the company being the center of attention, not the customer. Challenged to do so, they began to brainstorm first a drizzle of ideas, then a torrent. Excitement began to build as the people in the room saw how that simple shift in perspective — from "us" to "them" — could help the company differentiate itself from its competition and provide real value to the end users of their products. They were experiencing a Copernican shift in their outlook.

The shift isn't always an easy one to make, whether astronomical, personal or corporate in scope. Our natural tendency is to focus a microscope on ourselves instead of a telescope on others. The German poet Goethe understood how profoundly Copernicus had challenged that proclivity.

"Of all discoveries and opinions, none may have exerted a greater effect on the human spirit than the doctrine of Copernicus," he wrote. "The world had scarcely become known as round and complete in itself when it was asked to waive the tremendous privilege of being the center of the universe. Never, perhaps, was a greater demand made on mankind — for by this admission so many things vanished in mist and smoke! No wonder his contemporaries did not wish to let all this go . . ."

Many of your contemporaries do not wish to let it go, either. But if you're courageous enough to make the conceptual leap to a truly customer-centric system, a whole new world will be opened to you.

CUSTOMER-CENTRICITY

Jones Soda Co. offers a fascinating glimpse of that brave new world. It not only preaches customer-centricity, it practices it with literally every bottle of soda it sells — each is adorned with a picture of an actual customer. The company actively solicits customers to send in pictures of themselves to be featured on the bottles. For a small price, customers can even order entire cases with their specific photos stamped on the bottles.

That product offering is an outgrowth of Jones Soda's founding premise: the basic product formulation was not substantially different from its competitors (brand marketers take note!). Rather, it was the customer, the company determined, that was key. Jones actually put the customer in charge of the brand and allowed the customer to determine product strategy and product mix. Who else but a company like Jones Soda would market a product called "Turkey and Gravy" soda for Thanksgiving? Or put the customer front and center on the package?

"Our strategy is to develop unique brand names, slogans and trade dress," said founder Peter van Stolk. "We promote interaction with our customers through the use of posters, stickers, table cards, hats, pins, T-shirts and invite them to send in photographs to be used in packaging."

By putting the customer first, Jones Soda has created a very successful brand in the face of mega-brands Coke and Pepsi. Do you think they understand their customers?

Another forward-looking company is New Pig Corporation, which used some Copernican thinking to jazz up its line of cleaning products. Looking at it from the customer's vantage point, the company execs realized how dull and undifferentiated their image and products really were. So some marketing genius came up with the frankly wacky notion of putting pigs at the center of everything the company touches.

The company's address is on Pork Avenue. Its phone number is 1-800-HOT-HOGS. Its products feature the "boar facts" and offer "squeal for joy" service promises. There's even a company song that encourages people to "kiss a pig, hug a swine." New Pig branding is pervasive — and it all came from a realization that when looking at the company from the outside-in, the customer thought the product category dull and lifeless.

Has it worked? New Pig Corporation currently sells a line of over 2,500 products to 170,000 customers in more than 40 countries. The bottom line is that real growth happens when you take the time to look at your product offerings, brand and service structure through your customers' eyes, not yours.

On a more conventional note, let's take a look at Sysco, North America's largest food service distributor. A few years ago, the story goes, Sysco was conducting some fairly conventional customer research, in essence asking the restaurants that used its services, "What can we do better to serve you?" And, as so often happens in these cases, the company was getting some fairly conventional, and not particularly helpful, responses: "Give me my products cheaper, on time, with better quality, in the right amount."

(In my experience, asking questions like that is a waste of money. Very few customers can put your business out of their minds when answering. When asked questions about what you can do for them, most of your customers won't think past their most basic needs.)

But some customer-centric thinker over at Sysco wasn't satisfied with such pat answers. These were the table stakes that all customers expected, after all; there was no way to address them that would significantly budge the "customer needle." Then came the brainstorm.

Many of Sysco's customers were small restaurants whose owners did not have access to or completely understand certain industry best practices — practices, as it happened, that Sysco knew intimately: payroll, employee scheduling, tax reporting. By providing its customers with in-depth knowledge about these issues, Sysco would be providing real value beyond what was expected. Even better, as its restaurant customers accelerated their growth, they would in turn purchase more from Sysco.

The new customer-centric program proved a true win-win, exceeding Sysco's expectations. Just goes to show that a little customer focus is a good thing!

SEE YOURSELF AS OTHERS SEE YOU

To see ourselves as others see us is one of the most important habits we can acquire, both professionally and personally. It provides the impetus for positive change. Creating a true customer-centric organization begins with this outside-in perspective, a perspective that is itself formed through a process of constructive dialogue with your external stakeholders in order to better understand their needs.

All successful companies are, in the final analysis, customer-focused. For young companies, the main challenge is refining the accuracy of that focus; for more established companies, it's maintaining the discipline of that focus. Too often, businesses begin with the right mindset, but ironically success subverts it. There will always be the temptation to make your company the center of your corporate universe — resist it! Ego can kill the most successful enterprise (or individual, for that matter).

One of the hallmarks of good businesses — and good business leaders — is that they are always actively searching for ways to improve. Great companies seek this improvement through the eyes of their customers and stakeholders. And this isn't simply some kind of metaphysical mumbo-jumbo; the benefits of customer-centricity are eminently real: crystallization of your true customer base, identification of lucrative new revenue streams, development of high-return service offerings.

Customer-centric strategies aren't simply for theorists; properly executed, they almost invariably result in both top and bottom line growth. Isn't that worth a shift in perspective?

KEYS TO ACTION:

1. **Engage your entire organization.** If the customer is going to be the center of your organization's focus, everyone in the organization must be involved. Don't simply foist this off on the Sales and Marketing departments — getting Bob in Finance to understand your customers and their needs can just as easily provide a customer service breakthrough as the more traditional customer-facing areas. Your new customer-centric focus and solutions must pervade the entire company. In fact, many of the most exciting customer-oriented ideas derive from company-to-company "process" ideas, not simply new marketing campaigns or sales strategies.

2. **Employ third parties for research.** It's a fact that customers simply won't speak as frankly to an organization's employees as they will to a third party. Most will (sometimes even unconsciously) "dial back" their feedback to avoid confrontation or potential conflict. If you want the straight goods, you must employ a third party resource. The other reason to employ a third party is expertise — they know how to ask the right questions to get real insight.

3. **Use qualitative research techniques.** In my experience, quantitative research techniques just scratch the surface. To truly understand how the customer sees you, you should use more in-depth techniques like

ethnography, focus groups and one-on-one interviews. Use any technique that provides for real interaction, observation and communication. Because these tools are usually open-ended, they provide insights that draw from the totality of your customers' experiences, not just their experience with your specific products or services. That can give you an interesting perspective on category and service linkages you may have otherwise not considered.

4. **Walk a mile in your customer's shoes.** Consciously create situations that put you through the experience your customer is having with your organization. There is no better teacher than the negative experience you yourself might have through the process. Use "blind" techniques like mystery shoppers. Further, experience your own programs by assigning employees across functions to test them out independently and report back. You can even use role-playing within your organization to better see yourself through your customers' eyes.

5. **Talk most to the most dissatisfied customers.** Although it is the most difficult group to speak with, it is also the group from which you can learn the most. In fact, one company I know conducts all its customer research exclusively with its "dissatisfieds!" I don't agree completely with their logic, but it is certainly an interesting position.

Lessons From the Five and Dime
Improving your customer focus starts with your heart, not your head.

Every summer, my parents used to bundle the family into the car for our eagerly anticipated vacation to a rented cottage in lake country. We loved the wild beauty of the place, the feel that it was tucked into a little corner of the world that time had forgotten.

This was especially true of the picturesque little town nearby, where small mom-and-pop stores lined Main Street. And the best of the bunch was the local "five and dime," an eclectic little store called Joe's Emporium. Stepping into Joe's was an adventure. You didn't shop, you *explored*. I still remember the scents, a delightful blend of cotton candy, wood and machine oil that evoked something mysterious . . . something magical.

Joe was the most popular guy in town, always dressed in old jeans and a faded shirt, a smile perpetually on his face and twinkle in his eye. He had a memory like an elephant, always treating our family like old friends — even though he only saw us once a year. To my pre-adolescent mind, he was an almost mythic figure.

He ran his store just the way I imagined the people in those Norman Rockwell paintings would have. Doing business always played second fiddle to passing the time of day. When you walked through his door, he made you feel wanted. Liked. Trusted.

Somehow, Joe's Emporium made the world a nicer place to live. And so it's no surprise to me that his business continued to thrive long after the rest of the town's stores had succumbed to an invasion of the dreaded "big box" retailers. People just liked going to Joe's. It was more than a store; it was an oasis for the soul.

CHANGE OF HEART

Despite all the clamoring for more customer-centric business practices these days, the sad fact is that old Joe knew more about connecting with customers than most MBA grads will ever know. "Pay attention to your customer! Build customer experience!" the pundits cry. The good news is that more and more businesses are trying to do just that, trying to re-discover the Joe's Emporium within.

The bad news is that most businesses have no real clue how to do that. They've approached the problem with the collective corporate *head*, when what's really needed is a change of the corporate *heart*. Joe didn't treat his customers the way he did because of some formal mission statement on a 30-page business plan; he treated them that way because it was the right thing to do.

That's a tough morsel to digest for CEOs and business owners who depend on quantifiable metrics to gauge success and justify policies, and it's easy to understand why they focus so heavily on system-wide, process-driven reform. That's something tangible, something measurable. Something *real*. The personal touch that came so effortlessly to Joe seems, on the other hand, very intangible to the corporate mind.

For real change to take place, it has to start with the individual. Specifically, it has to start with the individual at the top of the organization and filter down to everyone else, gradually transforming attitudes and outlooks. Only then can behaviors change meaningfully. It's the old "practice what you preach" model. No corporate process, no management system, however well intentioned or strategically sound, can substitute for that.

That change of heart affects more than customer service, too. The real issue here is trust, whether it's trusting customers to give us their business or trusting our employees not to slack off or trusting our superiors not to steal credit for our ideas. Our parents taught us to not trust strangers; as adults we've learned to not trust anyone except a small group of friends and family. We've learned to keep our cards close to the vest, how to avoid being someone else's meal in this dog-eat-dog world, how to do unto others before they do unto us — and how to speak in bad clichés to avoid saying something genuine and true and vulnerable.

And because we've learned to do that, we've contributed to the general nastiness. Afraid to trust anyone, we inadvertently sow the seeds of mistrust. And those weeds have grown up thick and strong, choking our personal relationships and our business dealings. As hard as it is to admit it, we've become part of the problem even as we search for solutions.

Old Joe understood the solution, though. His approach to customer service was remarkable precisely because he didn't see it as "customer service." It was simply part and parcel of who he was, an extension of how he treated everyone in his life. We felt like long-lost friends when we walked in his shop because that's exactly how he would have treated actual long-lost friends.

The cure for mistrust is trust, and the only way to acquire trust is to first practice it.

IT'S A ROCKWELL WORLD AFTER ALL

I recently had another "Joe's Emporium" experience with my landlord. After 15 years, our house was starting to show some signs of age. My wife and I agreed to bite the bullet and do the dreaded house renovation. To save our sanity, we moved out while the repairs were underway, renting a house nearby so we could keep tabs on the project's progress.

During the renovation, we decided to replace most of our kitchen appliances, which, despite being pretty new and in excellent condition, didn't really fit the new scheme. I hit on the idea of trying to persuade our temporary landlord to take them off our hands for a reasonable sum, since the appliances in our rental home had definitely seen better days. In my mind, it was a win-win scenario.

I'd never met the landlord, only talked to him over the phone, so I'd mentally prepared all sorts of proof points and verification strategies to plead my case. But he surprised me. He listened quietly to my offer, then agreed to meet my price. He'd never met me face-to-face, never dealt with me before, never even seen the appliances in question. But he agreed!

I was flabbergasted. This guy was an experienced businessman, wise in the ways of the world, but he trusted me enough to take me at my word. Secretly, I felt more than a little chastened; in his place, I was forced to admit, I never would have had that kind of courage. I'd be too afraid of being taken advantage of.

But because he wasn't afraid to make himself vulnerable, I felt my own trust in him grow exponentially. Here was a man I wanted to do business with, a man I wouldn't hesitate to recommend to my friends and family. Like Old Joe, he put into practice what most of us are only willing to preach about.

And *that's* the kind of world I want to live in.

KEYS TO ACTION:

1. **To build your "heart-focused" customer plan, first make your perspective others-focused.** Build your "Copernican thinking," consciously adjusting your worldview so that you "revolve" around others rather than assume that they revolve around you. You can start now by imagining how others see your dealings with them. What are their concerns? You'll be surprised at the options that open themselves to you and your business when you employ this type of approach.

2. **Practice "outside-in" thinking with your team.** Role-play. Expand this others-focused mentality to your co-workers and employees. One individual or group should play the part of the customers while others play "company" roles. By working through mock scenarios in this way, you'll accelerate the transformation of behavior and reinforce attitude with instinct.

3. **Begin with the assumption of trust.** Both Joe and my landlord started with trust and worked from there — a phenomenal accomplishment in today's cynical society. If you're not ready to take that big a step with strangers, that's OK. Start small. What would happen if you began showing some trust in your kids' judgment rather than questioning it?

4. **Be prepared to be burned once in a while.** Your kids won't always justify your trust. Customers and vendors won't always be straight with you. Don't let that discourage you, though. Most people will repay trust with trust.

5. **Be a role model.** Nobody's going to follow if no one is leading. You have to walk the talk to inspire others. Taking the first step toward improving your customer focus starts with yours truly.

6. **Reward appropriate behavior.** If you see it, reward it. Nothing will transform faster than appropriate behavior, appropriately and visibly rewarded. If they see it, they will come.

DWYSYWD
(Do What You Say You Will Do)

It's no secret that broken customer expectations are the root cause of most business failure. If you do only one thing, make sure it's delivering on your promises at all cost.

Once upon a time, a farmer and his wife had everything they could wish for . . . except children. The couple begged for a child, even if it was a hedgehog. The following year, his wife did indeed give birth to a son, whom they called Hans. But although the boy looked normal from the waist down, his upper half was that of a hedgehog. Eventually his parents grew tired of the strange boy, and Hans traveled to a distant forest. There he sat in a tree playing his flute.

Several years later, two kings became lost while hunting in that same forest. They heard music and followed it to none other than Hans the Hedgehog. Maintaining their royal composure, the kings explained their situation. Hans offered to show them each the way home in exchange for giving him anything he asked for. They both readily agreed.

True to his promise, Hans showed the kings the path out of the forest . . . and then demanded to marry each king's daughter. Nodding, the kings hastened back to the safety of their castles. There, the first king told the princess of his encounter in the forest and the strange creature's demand. But he reassured her that he had no intention of keeping his word.

The second king also told his daughter that she must also refuse. "No, father," she replied. "For your sake I will keep the promise you made."

Months later, Hans visited the first king's castle. He leapt over the guards and landed on the king's window ledge. "Give me what you promised," he cried, "or I will take your life."

Reluctantly, the princess agreed to go with him. But once outside the town, Hans stuck her with his quills and said, "That is your reward for breaking your promise!" And he left her there, publicly shamed.

Then Hans went to the second king, where he found an honor guard with orders to escort him to the palace. The princess was horrified at his appearance, but she greeted him warmly and the two were married that same day.

That night, she could not hide her fear. "Don't worry," Hans told her, and suddenly his hedgehog skin fell off. Under it, she saw the most handsome young man she had ever seen. "You have kept your promise," he told her. "And I am your reward." The princess was overjoyed, and she and Hans lived happily ever after. The moral of the story: do what you say you will do and you will be justly rewarded for your effort.

HOW HIGH IS TOO HIGH?

Business success, whether corporate or individual, is predicated on delivering the goods on time and in a quality fashion. It's the most important ingredient in establishing trust between two parties, whether customer and supplier or boss and employee. It's also one of the easiest rules to violate, whether intentionally or through inattention.

Henry used to run a very large portion of a packaged goods business for me a few years ago. He had a very interesting view of how to motivate his team to deliver results: he liked to set very aggressive goals, believing that in doing so he motivated the team to set their sights higher and work harder. Setting "stretch targets" is nothing new, of course, and by and large is a good thing . . . provided that the stretch wasn't out of reach.

That wasn't Henry's philosophy, however, as I discovered during our annual planning process. Henry's division had historically delivered top line annual growth of between three and five percent — not bad for a fairly mature grocery business. So I was, ah . . . *intrigued*, to read that he was committing to an extraordinary 25 percent growth for the coming year.

I read through Henry's plan with interest, eventually concluding that despite some innovative new thoughts on products and business processes, there was far less than a 50/50 chance he would achieve even half the growth the plan predicted. Needless to say, prior to a formal presentation of the plan to our superiors, I wanted to have a little chat with Henry to understand his thinking.

We met the next day and Henry laid out his rationale. He believed that in order to break free from the perils of incremental thinking, he had to get his group thinking outside the box. (In this, I think he was absolutely correct.) He thought that if he set a dramatic "motivational" goal of 25 percent but only achieved say, 17 percent, his division would still have more than tripled its historical annual growth rate.

It's an interesting tactic, to be sure. I tried to impress upon Henry, though, that while I respected his zeal, his plan bordered on the irresponsible (I resisted the impulse to say that it bordered on the insane). Were I, as his boss, to bank on his promise to deliver 25 percent top line growth, with a commensurate improvement in the bottom line, we would be forced to accept an inordinate amount of aggregate risk. What ensued was a philosophical discussion on leadership. Which was better — to set a challenging but historically achievable target, or to set an unprecedented target to build break-out growth? Was it better to deliver some extraordinary results and surpass historical performance but miss the mark on the formal commitment? Is the commitment more important than the improved result? Henry and I couldn't see eye-to-eye on the issue. Missing plan, in my view, was in fact failing to deliver on a commitment. Regardless of how well the division might have done compared to past growth, I felt that if I accepted the 25 percent target (and the spending associated with it) and we fell short, our commitments in aggregate would have missed plan.

In this example, I overruled Henry, accepting a lower growth objective for plan purposes while encouraging him to continue to push the team towards a higher, more inspirational goal. It turned out to be a win-win, allowing Henry and his team to deliver on their commitment while still striving for the stratosphere. (Later that year, he was also much happier with his bonus than he might have been if he had followed his original inclinations.) What would you have done?

GETTING THE JOB DONE

On the other end of the spectrum, my friend Duncan is steadfast about delivering on his promises, whatever the cost. He doesn't just talk the talk; he walks the walk. Consider this story:

Duncan owns a very successful printing business that depends heavily on printing annual reports for several large multinationals.

When he was just starting out, it wasn't uncommon for him to work seven days a week to ensure that his customers were satisfied. Finally, after more than a year of keeping his nose to the grindstone, Duncan decided to take a vacation to spend some much needed time with his family. They decided to pull out the stops and take one of those once-in-a-lifetime type trips to Disney World; the kids would have the run of the park, and he and his wife could find some time for themselves.

As the day of the trip drew closer, Duncan and his family grew more and more excited. Discussions around the dinner table focused almost exclusively on the upcoming vacation: the sights each of them planned to see, the rides they wanted to ride, even the restaurants they wanted to try. Then, the day before they were scheduled to leave, Duncan received a bombshell at work.

One of his employees had promised a major customer that their annual report would be printed and delivered to them the following day. Normally that wouldn't have been an issue, but the printing press malfunctioned and wouldn't be repaired in time to meet the deadline. There was no way that Duncan's facility would be able to fulfill the order.

Duncan faced a real dilemma. On the one hand, he knew that the customer didn't really need the report delivered on the day specified; a delay of a few days would make no difference to their plans. On the other hand, though, he knew that unless he stepped in personally — which would almost certainly affect his big vacation — to find a solution, his company would have failed to deliver on its commitment. What to do?

There was never a question in Duncan's mind, which shows you the kind of dedicated businessman he is. He cancelled his flight and told his family to go on without him. Then he called a few of his competitors, explained the situation and asked for their help. One of the companies agreed to free up their presses for Duncan's job, and within 24 hours the annual reports were in his customer's hands as promised. Duncan joined his family in Florida with a clean conscience. Perhaps even more impressively, Duncan never told the customer about the hoops he'd had to jump through, delaying his trip and actually losing money on the job because of the change in printing venue.

There is a post-script, though. Duncan's customer eventually did discover the diligence with which Duncan he had fulfilled his commitment. They were so impressed that they went out of their way to recommend him to others, and Duncan's business took off.

The lesson is simple: DWYSYWD and you will be rewarded.

OVER-DELIVER

Home renovation. These two words alone can cause knees to buckle and spines to shiver. Why? Because you can probably count on one hand the number of people who have been through a home renovation without some kind of screw-up, delay, complication or crisis. And most of them stem from contractors and subcontractors making commitments and then breaking them.

It's all about that initial expectation. Say that a prospective contractor comes to you and swears that your renovation will be completed in three months; most of the other contractors you talk to tell you that six months is the absolute minimum. You swallow your misgivings, hire the guy . . . and the work is completed in four months. Now are you happy that he finished two months ahead of the "norm," or miffed that he broke his promise?

Consider another approach. Our golf course was inundated a year ago by a freak flood and needed substantial repairs. The board met and concluded that the best option was to shut down the course for the remainder of the year and do the job right. They arranged for alternate playing time at neighboring clubs and communicated the plan to the membership, who endorsed the proposal.

Repairs ended up progressing more quickly than expected, and the course was reopened ahead of schedule in early October. It remained open until late November, when winter weather put an end to golf season in these parts. The membership received two months of play on their own course they hadn't anticipated — and, needless to say, they let the board know their appreciation.

The board could have taken a different route. When they made their decision, they knew that there was a chance — even a good chance — that the course might be reopened that same year. But they knew that was better to set a realistic expectation and then over-deliver than risk the ire of the membership by setting what could have been an overly aggressive target in the first place and then falling short.

In the end, it's all about setting the right expectation — and then delivering on it.

KEYS TO ACTION:

1. **Start by putting yourself in your customer's shoes.** Ask yourself: What are their expectations? To whom are they making commitments, and how do these dovetail into what you have committed? How important is the

commitment? Is it major or minor? How is the commitment likely to impact the organization or individuals within it if it is missed? What's the downside?

2. **Make the commitment realistic.** If your goals are too low, it will become clear that you're sandbagging; too high and you'll only be setting yourself up to fail. Instead, choose the middle road, one that offers value but is still attainable within the timeframe specified.

3. **Consider the impact of not fulfilling your promise.** The essential thing here is to look at failure from a 360-degree perspective. How will it impact not only your customer, but also their customers? What about your own team members and other external stakeholders?

4. **Track your progress and provide regular updates to your stakeholders.** Doing so helps keep the project front and center and avoids costly surprises and the dreaded "mission creep."

5. **Communicate good news quickly and bad news faster.** You don't necessarily have to have a solution, but you must at least demonstrate that you've considered alternative solutions. To do otherwise is to throw the monkey on someone else's back, which does no good for anyone — particularly your reputation.

Moving Targets

As soon as you think you know who your target customer is, you don't — they change. Lead your customers or they'll quickly outgrow you.

It's hard to believe in this age of satellite mapping and handheld GPS technology, but it wasn't that long ago that sailors venturing beyond sight of land were launching themselves into the great unknown. The risk was enough to chill most landsman; the eighteenth century English essayist Samuel Johnson once famously remarked that it was preferable to be in prison than at sea; the quarters and food were much the same, and at least in prison you stood no chance of drowning.

If anything, Johnson may have underestimated the rigors of an ocean voyage. Starvation, thirst and scurvy were equally great threats to sailors as drowning; a ship that missed its landfall could run desperately short of food and water, its crew dying slowly and agonizingly. Or it could run aground on reefs, marooning its crew on hostile or unknown shores with little chance of rescue.

Accurate navigation was essential, but that was easier said than done. There were two methods: celestial navigation, which used the positions of the sun, moon and stars to fix the location of the ship; and rule of thumb navigation, in which the sailing master or captain used the compass and logline (which indicated the speed of the ship) to estimate distance and direction traveled. Many old school mariners preferred rule of thumb navigation. But more scientifically minded sailors knew it had one great failing: it could not anticipate the tides.

In fact, the ocean is in constant motion, and for every nautical mile a ship traveled in a certain direction, it was also sliding off-course due to the effect of wind and the moon's gravitational field. Even a small variance could be devastating, particularly over a long journey — you might end up hundreds of miles from where you thought you were, with both crew and supplies exhausted, or crash into a shore you believed was safely in the distance.

Only by understanding tidal movement and compensating for it using celestial navigation could you reliably reach your intended destination. Anything else, it soon became clear, was not only ineffective — it was sheer madness.

INNOVATORS, LAGGARDS AND EVERYONE IN BETWEEN

Like the tides, your customers are in constant motion. Unless you compensate, you're likely in for some very unpleasant surprises. Unfortunately, most customer research conducted with your primary target group is like looking through a rear view mirror. It shows you not where they're going, but either where they are right at this moment or, even worse, where they've been. If you're simply reacting to that information instead of anticipating what's to come, you will find yourself at the back of the pack when it comes to leadership in your industry.

Where will your customers be tomorrow? Next month? Next year? The odds indicate that they won't be where they are now. They are constantly evolving, and it's your job to not only keep pace, but to stay ahead of them.

In technology circles it's known as the "Innovator's Dilemma." Do you trash what you've created to introduce something better, or do you max out the current technology before moving on.

Microsoft, to give you one example, tends to favor the latter approach, while Apple has embraced the former, changing the rules of the game to stay ahead of the competition while they're still struggling to catch up with the last product. Just consider the success of the iPhone. Apple's competitors by now all have their own knock-offs of the popular iPod, so Apple opted to change the paradigm. Apple understands that frequent innovation — even more frequent than is required — is the way to maintain market leadership. (For a more detailed discussion about market leadership, see the chapter titled "King of the Hill.")

One of the most important lessons I've learned in the creation of compelling customer communication is that it is essential to provide your customers with new ideas. It's not your customer's job to be a pioneer — it's yours. You must help prospects see your offering in a new light. You must add to their reservoir of knowledge.

I recently did a study of over 50 CEOs to discover the "best in class" as it relates to customer top-to-tops. (A top-to-top is a meeting held between the respective heads of customer and supplier organizations, usually to review the state of the relationship and the business.) The organization that commissioned my work was interested in how they could change their meeting process to deliver the best, most effective top-to-top meetings with their customers. The findings were instructive; the CEOs had very firm ideas about what works:

- Spend at least 75 percent of the meeting listening, not talking.
- When you do talk, focus on the customer, not you. ("Copernican" thinking again).

- Most importantly, *teach them something new*. All the CEOs I interviewed said that they considered a meeting successful if they learned something new during the meeting itself, something they could take back to their organizations.

Most of you are probably familiar with the Rogers Adoption/Innovation Schematic, which has long been a tried and trusted tool for marketing types. It describes the process through which a new product or idea moves into market. According to this model, there are five customer segments that are ready to "consume" at different points in a product's life cycle:

- **Stage 1: Innovators (2.5%).**
  These customers are the bleeding edge, the risk-takers willing and eager to try the newest technologies and ideas.
- **Stage 2: Early Adopters (13.5%).**
  These people are ahead of the curve.
- **Stage 3: Early Majority (34%).**
  The front half of mainstream users.
- **Stage 4: Late Majority (34%).**
  The back half of mainstream users.
- **Stage 5: Laggards (16%).**
  By the time these folks adopt a product, it's already almost obsolete.

Here's my twist on the model: *In order to lead your customer, focus on the group that is at least one step ahead of where you believe the majority of your customers to be.* For example, if you are a relatively mature business, it's likely that most of your customer base is composed of Early or Late Majority segments. In order to lead your customers, focus on the group just ahead of them — in this case, the Early Adopters. Talk to them. Get to know them. Use them to shape your ideas and they'll help you better lead your mainstream customers.

YOUR CUSTOMERS AREN'T WHO YOU THINK THEY ARE

Here's a hard lesson from my past that demonstrates the danger of aiming at your customer instead of ahead of them:

Kraft Dinner is a Canadian food icon and holds a revered place in the hearts of most Canadians. Believe it or not, every Canadian eats the equivalent of about three boxes of the nuclear orange-colored Mac 'n Cheese product every year. In fact, it's the largest selling grocery SKU (Stock Keeping Unit) in the country!

For years, it was primarily targeted at pre-teen kids, advertised as the "cheesiest" Mac 'n Cheese on the market. In the early 90s, J.W. Thompson created what I considered to be some of the strongest advertising for the product yet. The spot showed unbelievably cute kids eating KD in various childish ways, all set to the tune of the song, "It Had To Be You."

Both the Kraft marketing people and the ad agency loved the spot. We paraded it for everyone to see and puffed up our chests, expecting big returns. But after running for a number of weeks, the business needle moved not one inch. We increased our advertising spend. Again, nothing. Despite our great hopes, the advertising was doing nothing for the business. What was going on?

Perplexed, we went back to the drawing board to try to understand where we went wrong. We ran focus groups among all kinds and ages of people. We looked into people's houses to try and understand how the product fit within their lives.

What we discovered was that we'd completely missed the target. *We'd aimed at our target group instead of leading them.* Turns out that the leading consumers of Kraft Dinner were not little kids — they were college students! As a result, KD was linked in most people's minds to that critical rite of passage: living away from home for the first time.

We also discovered that the product was most often remembered in pretty "unique" circumstances: eaten cold, snacked on when it was already several days old, combined with other foods to create some, uh . . . *interesting* dishes. Some folks even considered it a major food group!

No wonder we hadn't hit the mark. Cute kids playing with their food, while descriptive of who we thought was our primary user, didn't "lead" consumers to the product. We redirected our communication strategy accordingly and were rewarded with tremendous growth. (Interestingly, the new approach worked with all age groups. Older customers reacted nostalgically to the memory-evoking images; younger age groups began associating the food with "cool" older teens.) The incident became a lesson to me of the importance of staying ahead of the curve and leading your mainstream customers.

LEADING YOUR TARGET CONSUMERS

Here are two very important lessons to guide you as you shape a "leading" customer strategy.

First, *never underestimate the intelligence of your target customers.* Don't talk down to them, talk up. Your customer is a lot smarter than you may think. Even the appearance of condescension can do irreversible harm to the relationship. Few people are insulted if you treat them as more intelligent, discerning or knowledgeable than they really are. Aim one step higher than you think you should and you should hit your mark.

Secondly, *never ask your customers to design something new.* That's not their job and, quite frankly, they stink at it. Most customers' experiences are limited to what you already provide, so they will tend to give you only variations on that theme. Put it another way: they see you for what you are, not what you could be.

The lesson: ask your customers to react to ideas, not to build them.

KEYS TO ACTION:

1. **Use your lead customers to drive your in-market execution.** They set the pace for those who follow. Talk to them, learn about their preferences, wants and needs. Walk a mile in their shoes. By building programming that meets the needs of these customers, you will ensure that you keep on the leading edge of the adoption curve, instead of getting stuck in the meaty middle.

2. **When in doubt, aim higher and act sooner.** It is more dangerous to underestimate your customer base that it is to overestimate it, more dangerous to act too slowly than too rapidly. It's rare that you will go wrong acting too quickly on a piece of information.

3. **Talk to the right people.** Canvass your front line employees on a regular basis to ensure that you are speaking with the "right" customers and to help identify possible changes in marketplace dynamics. Create a system for ongoing customer dialogue. Even reach out to leading customers in like industries to provide context and flavor.

4. **Build a database of dissatisfied customers.** Sometimes the best lessons come from people who aren't enamored with you. Learn from these people what you or your company does not do well, or how you are failing to adequately address their needs. What you discover will likely be more instructive than what you learn from your biggest fans.

5. **Hire soothsayers.** There is value in listening to people who focus on trends for a living, but be selective and sensible about what advice you take. You've got to temper "bleeding edge" with where you stand as an industry and a company. If you are a mainstream company, for instance, don't just jump on the latest trend.

6. **Let your lead customers speak for you.** There can be strength in letting your best customers lead your other customers. Show them in your communication and ask them to speak on your behalf. Because they are leaders in their own right, they can inspire their peers and colleagues to want to emulate them.

Exorcizing Demon Customers

Customers are not all created equal. In fact, 20 percent of yours are responsible for 80 percent of your pain. Get rid of 'em!

When *The Exorcist* debuted in movie theatres in 1973, it was hailed as the scariest film ever made. Some moviegoers literally fainted from fright and needed paramedic assistance. One man passed out and broke his jaw on the seat in front of him. He sued the studio, which settled out of court. Other theaters, schooled by experience, began providing "Exorcist barf bags" for patrons. (Author's note: Great marketing!)

For me, one of the most frightening scenes was the first encounter with the possessed girl. Two priests enter her bedroom apprehensively and find it as frigid as a Siberian winter morning. Standing on either side of her bed, their exhaled breath visibly crystallizes in the freezing air. The girl herself lies on her bed, her eyes closed. She seems peaceful and innocent, the very image of childlike beauty. How could she be possessed? Surely this must be a mistake . . .

Slowly her eyes open, red and bloodshot and gleaming with evil amusement. Suddenly, a stream of gibberish erupts from her mouth, a torrent of dead and clipped English profanity. Her body trembles and shakes. Her head slowly turns to the right, spewing curses on the priests. To their shock and fear, it completes a full revolution. There can be no doubt that this is evil ancient and incarnate, and the two priests visibly brace themselves for the ordeal ahead.

Sure sounds like a couple of customers I know.

AN EVIL MYTH

For most of us, "demon" customers are much harder to identify than the possessed girl in *The Exorcist*. As a rule, they don't projectile vomit a geyser of pea-green puke (although dealing with them may make *you* want to throw up). Their heads don't spin round (although you may want to wring their necks on occasion). They don't speak in tongues (although they'll have you spewing a torrent of profanity behind their back).

The unfortunate reality is that most demon customers, on the surface, seem like everyone else. In fact, they may themselves be unaware of their true nature. But demon customers exist, you've probably got 'em, and even as we speak they may be sucking the lifeblood out of your company. The sooner you are able identify and exorcise them, the sooner your business will benefit.

Easier said than done, right? A while back, I stared across a conference table at a group of radio executives and wondered how to tell them that the last national account they had scored was a loser. These were hard-knock sales folks who knew their industry and knew how to chase down leads and convert them into time blocks sold. For years, their philosophy had been "any customer is a good customer." It was my unenviable task to educate them that this old truism was not, in fact, true.

Their situation wasn't unique. Years before, I had assumed the leadership of another business organization that had developed along similar lines. Culturally, the group had bought into the notion that the bigger the customer, the better. Not only did they bring in money, they also provided a certain cache simply by being a customer — that would, reasoned the groupthink, surely bring in even more big customers.

That organization had succumbed to an evil myth. Not only is bigger not necessarily better, in most cases we discovered that these mega-customers were actually bad for business. (I know. It didn't make sense to them, either — at first.) To prove it, I conducted a customer profitability study that forced us to take an inventory of all of our customer-related costs and where they were being applied.

I have often had the occasion to cast my eyes upward and give thanks for the folks from the finance department. This was one of those times. They performed a bottom-up exercise called "activity-based costing" that aligned the right costs to the right customers. Before that, costs had been averaged out across the customer base in the belief that it provided a decent view of the costs associated with each customer. As it turns out, that was a fundamentally flawed belief.

What emerged from this financial exercise was a very different view of the customer base. To widespread surprise, we saw that some of our largest customers were actually our "worst" profit performers. They sucked vital resources in terms of the people dedicated to the business, they were the most demanding in terms of price concessions, and they were quite low on business sustainability. They regularly required us to bid on projects, which resulted in more time and resources spent preparing the bid as well as the inevitable price concessions. (Think about it: when was the last time *you* were able to increase price and build margin through an RFP process?)

This fact-based educational process proved invaluable in shifting the corporate culture concerning customers.

We initiated rolling seminars and self-paced, Internet-based sessions to help our employees (all of them, not just the sales or finance departments) understand the new customer profitability information. Meanwhile, a smaller group delved deep into the customer information we had gleaned, creating a new segmentation and pricing model. "Gold" customers had a set of profit and strategic characteristics that made them most attractive. "Silver" and "Bronze" customers were less desirable.

The object was not necessarily to have only "Gold" customers — that, frankly, would have been unrealistic — but to be able to marry pricing and resources utilized in a way that maximized our return. To make sure this customer world-view became ingrained in our corporate culture, we even created case studies and used role-playing exercises.

All that in place, we rewrote our customer plans and, believe me, they looked very different than they had. In some cases this new segmentation led to some difficult conversations with customers that had benefited from the cost "averaging." In essence, they had been net users of our resources; to restore the balance, they had to be "de-serviced." Some were cooperative, some were furious, and we even lost a few.

The result? Within two years of the retooling, we tripled our margin and doubled our profit . . . while actually reducing our top line!

SEGMENTATION SUCCESS

No doubt many of you are familiar with Pareto's Principle. It states that 80 percent of the benefits accrue as a result of only 20 percent of the base. This 80/20 rule is usually the case with your customer base as well, with 80 percent of your revenue coming from 20 percent of your customers. Well, here's Hunter's

Corollary to Pareto's Principle: *20 percent of your customer base creates about 80 percent of your pain.* Within that 20 percent lie your demon customers.

Before you exorcize them, though, you've got to first figure out who they are. Some signs are obvious. They enjoy "kicking the tires" in an attempt to extort price concessions from you. Customer loyalty counts for little; they're perfectly willing to shop around before every purchase for the best price. In fact, price is usually their primary criterion, trumping service or other value-adds. They are the cherry pickers, here today for a big discount and gone tomorrow.

Sound familiar? Chances are you've got customers like these. Find them, see them for what they are and get rid of them. And don't skimp on the holy water!

Customer segmentation is the best and most reliable method of identifying these problem-causers. Remember the radio station preoccupied with big national accounts? With my help, they developed a customer segmentation process that helped them spot real strategic customers, the ones with the best growth potential (and therefore also the ones most able to spend more money in radio advertising down the road). This system allowed the station to flag a select few businesses that warranted additional "investment," including a program that invited these business owners to regular retreats where they could receive one-on-one consulting from subject area experts about how to build their businesses and implement efficient processes.

Thanks to this value-add service that benefited both the radio station's customers and the station itself, profits increased and expenses decreased — and the station's reputation soared as it never had when its sales force was focused on wooing high-profile customers.

Once you've identified your demon customers, you've got to rid yourself of them. How? Simple, actually. First, plan for their exit. The loss of any customers will create excess capacity in your organization, which must be either redeployed or reduced (downsizing your workforce, your resource allocation or both). In the case of customer contracts, timing is an issue. Map out expirations for the coming 12 months.

Most of the time, your customers will self-select as you price up or "service down." The most important thing is to make the process visible to them (and to your own organization) and to stay committed to your program. Nothing will sabotage your exorcism efforts more than the example of a customer that escaped the purge. Remember the old saying: "You can bend on a practice, but not on a principle." This is a principle.

The few that don't self-select must be "managed out." This can be a delicate procedure; your goal is to leave them with the feeling that they controlled the exit process, not you. Stay the course and you'll be amazed at how quickly those customers are forgotten and how quickly your business will improve as a result.

Exorcize your demon customers!

KEYS TO ACTION:

1. **Conduct a review of your current resources and their allocation across the activity of your organization and your customer base.** This activity-based costing exercise will give you real visibility of your profitability, customer by customer.

2. **Segment your customer base into zones of profitability.** These natural groupings will form the base for your resource segmentation and your future customer strategy.

3. **Allow for a special grouping of "strategically important" customers.** These may not be the most profitable customers, but they are strategic imperatives. Maintain a firm hand when determining the rationale for this grouping — it is easy to become lenient and water down the reason for the group.

4. **Communicate your new customer strategy within your organization.** Link your measurement and compensation systems to the new program. Involve your team, particularly those who are customer-facing, in customer analysis and customer strategy redevelopment. Reinforce their participation with appropriate rewards.

5. **Identify actions to take with each customer grouping.** Keep a special eye on those customers you want to wean from your business. Deal with the bottom-feeders first to immediately free up additional resources to help support your more profitable customers.

The Exhibitionist

Show 'em, don't tell 'em. Proof — not words — turns skeptics into believers and prospects into customers.

During the golden age of the infomercial in the 1980s and 90s, you couldn't turn on late night television without encountering Ron Popeil. Part inventor, part Atlantic City boardwalk huckster, Popeil became famous for his animated demonstrations of gadgets like the Veg-O Matic food slicer, the Popeil Pocket Fisherman, Mr. Microphone, the Inside-the-Shell Egg Scrambler, GLH-9 Hair in a Can Spray, the Smokeless Ashtray and the Electric Food Dehydrator.

The gadgets were frequently silly, but Popeil's approach was carefully thought out and polished. He backed up his outrageous product claims with demonstrations that drew gasps, cheers and applause from the audience — and then he wowed them some more. And who could argue with him? After all, we'd seen the success of his inventions with our own eyes.

Thanks to his seeing-is-believing sales pitch, Popeil made a fortune hawking a never-ending stream of cheesy products. Advertised in print, it's unlikely that he would have made enough to buy a used car, but Popeil understood the power of a visual medium like TV — and the even greater power of show, don't tell.

Popeil sold his company, Ronco, in 2005 for $55 million. Think there's no profit in being an exhibitionist? Think again.

PROOF POSITIVE

Car dealerships can be a squirrelly bunch.

Over the years, I've had occasion to offer several of them marketing advice on how to differentiate themselves from the guy next door, which is obviously a major concern for them in attracting prospective buyers. Our conversations almost always went something like this:

Me: "Tell me what makes you different from your competitors."

Dealer: "Our exceptional service."

Me: "OK, how do I know that your service is really better than Joe's Car Dealership down the street?"

Dealer: "We just are."

Me: "Sigh."

(In fairness, sometimes their answers vary. I've also heard "Ask our customers and they'll tell you" and "We've been in business for so many years that we must be doing something right.")

What they failed to see was that their pat answers wouldn't move my "desire to purchase" needle one iota — or yours either, I'm willing to bet. Telling me does nothing, especially when I've heard it before; actually showing me proves everything. P.T. Barnum was not the most scrupulous businessman, but he understood like few others the power of demonstration. Talking about the Fiji Mermaid was one thing, actually putting her on display in a tank for all to see was quite another.

So I gently suggested to one of these dealers that simply talking about service wasn't as effective as demonstrating it. Imagine if, I told him, one Saturday morning you open your door for the morning paper and find on your doorstep instead a couple of bright-eyed college kids in coveralls with the dealer's logo on them. They tell you that the dealer has implemented a program to thank its customers for their continued support, so they're to wash the car you bought from them two years ago . . . free of charge. Would that make an impact on you? What if a few teams like this, driving dealer-branded vans and wearing dealer-branded shirts, randomly washed cars for existing customers all over town? Would that get people talking about the dealer's "exceptional service?" Damn right it would.

We live in a jaded, cynical world. How many TV commercials have you seen advertising the best service, the best price, the best quality? How many have you really believed? Yeah, me too. The fact is, we've heard it all before. And almost always the next big thing turns out to be just one more thing. It's tiring — show me or shut up.

There are a few exceptions, and they stand out. Procter and Gamble is diligent in providing some sort of product demonstration or other concrete proof. Crest toothpaste backs up its cavity-prevention claims with dentist testimonials and smiling, cavity-free children. Head & Shoulders shampoo ensures that you see absolutely no dandruff on a dark sweater after someone has shaken their hair. The list goes on.

Procter wrote the book on developing a compelling creative strategy: 1) identify the consumer issue; 2) show how "product X" resolves the issue. Pretty simple, eh?

Product or service demonstrations don't have to break the bank, either, as some people seem to think. In fact, it's often the small ideas that pack the biggest punch. I've seen service-savvy car dealerships, for example, use some of these effective but inexpensive "shows":

- Placing a fresh cut flower on the passenger seat following servicing of the vehicle for every woman who brings her car in.
- Designating a couple of car bays as "female friendly." These areas are painted differently, kept clean and staffed by females. (I even saw one car repair shop that positioned itself as a ladies-only shop. Hey, if Curves can do it, why not?)
- Offering free pick-up and delivery service. You just throw them the keys and your car is whisked away and returned magically when servicing is completed.
- Free "fills." The car is returned with a full tank of gas, and all other fluid levels are checked and topped off.

Simple, eh? But very, very effective.

SHOW IT TO SELL IT

Think back to the last time you wandered through a food or consumer trade show. As you perused the various booths, you undoubtedly ran smack dab into my favorite form of huckster: a Popeil wannabe on slightly raised stage sporting a crisp apron and holding a microphone.

"Ladies and gentlemen," runs the standard opening. "How many of you are sick and tired of spending hours cutting, slicing and dicing vegetables? Me too! (Insert joke here to warm up audience.) I'm here today to show you the most amazing discovery since man invented the wheel. Yes sir, after today, you're going to be able to throw away those paring knives. This magical little machine will not only slice, dice . . ."

Know what I'm talking about? It's actually a little mesmerizing. At first, only a few people stop and stare, but if the presenter is any good at all, by the time the show is in full swing there's a major crowd. We're all interested, and what's more, we *know* we're being sold. And we love it.

Pretty soon the crowd begins oohing and aahing as our little ringleader puts the machine through its paces. Sure enough, it seems to do all that's promised. The presenter ends with a call to action — usually some sort of special offer — and the bystanders start diving for their wallets. Seeing the product with their own eyes removed doubts and galvanized their desire to buy.

There used to be a company (the farthest thing from Procter you can get in terms of class) that was a master at this type of hype: K-Tel. I imagine many of us over the age of 45 probably have a streak of nostalgia for the Winnipeg-based company and its "But wait, there's more!" slogan from the 60s. The first really well-known "as-seen-on-TV" company, K-Tel sold a bewildering spread of wacky and dubious products: the Fishin' Magician, the Buttonmatic, the Patty Stacker, the Brush-O-Magic, the Hair Magician and the ever-famous K-Tel record selector. If K-Tel's success isn't proof that demonstration can sell just about anything, I don't know what is.

Today, The Shopping Network uses a more upscale and contemporary version of this "show it to sell it" strategy, but the fundamental principles are the same. We've even begun to see this approach successfully used in other business arenas such as recruiting. The rage now is "behavioral interviewing," which is really just a fancy name for requiring a prospective candidate to provide proof to back up claims of particular competencies. Let's say that a prospective candidate says that she has exceptional leadership skills. OK, says the interviewer, tell me about three occasions on which you demonstrated this "exceptional leadership" and why you believe it was exceptional. As with product demonstrations, behavioral interviewing is pretty simple — but it's also pretty effective. Studies show that it's a good indicator of a new hire's success or failure.

Hamlet wanted the "ocular proof" before he was willing to act to revenge his father's death. Your customers, whatever your industry, want ocular proof as well before they're willing to engage your services or buy your products. Don't keep them waiting — give it to them!

KEYS TO ACTION:

1. **Focus on your point of differentiation.** What sets your product, service or company apart from your competition? Once you've determined what that is, you must focus on demonstrating only that benefit or attribute.

2. **Brainstorm how to visually support the benefit via demonstration.** People have to see to believe. There are always a number of ways to "prove" your point of differentiation, but the idea here is that the more ways you can think of, the more interesting your whole story will become across your mix of marketing channels. Remember, though: "All roads must lead to that one compelling benefit."

3. **Choose demonstrations that compel and surprise.** The more outlandish the demonstration, the better — it creates interest and drives the message home. Gevalia coffee ran a series of stunts to support their tag line "for when people drop in unexpectedly." The "unexpected" events came in the form of things like a fake submarine "surfacing" from a downtown street. Absolutely brilliant, and very successful.

4. **Test the demonstration with your target group.** You've got to make sure the demo has the right impact on the right people. There's a fabulous (probably apocryphal) story about Procter conducting a demo for one of their products. They washed one duck with their product, another with a competitor's product. The duck that had been washed with the competitor's product actually sank! Although Procter's duck did just fine, the company chose not to run the ad and risk offending animal lovers.

5. **Track the effectiveness of your demonstrations.** Pre-testing is one thing, ongoing measurement another. You've got to keep a handle on the program's effectiveness over time. Executions can wear out, and they can react differently even if you've pre-tested.

6. **Show 'em, don't just tell 'em.** Don't talk about quality. Prove it. Don't speak of service. Show it. Done correctly, exhibitionism grows businesses.

The Razor's Edge

If you want to get, you first have to give. Win customers' trust — and their business — by demonstrating the value of your offering risk-free.

Back in the 1890s, a traveling salesman in the U.S. Midwest named King Gillette grew frustrated with the time and expense of having to continually sharpen his razor. What if the blade could be manufactured so inexpensively that it could simply be discarded when it became dull and replaced with a new one in the same holder?

Convinced he had a million-dollar idea, Gillette spent the next five years overcoming technological obstacles. In fact, it was 1903 before his first disposable safety razors debuted on the market. Having invested both his time and his hard-earned money, he waited anxiously for the profits to roll in.

He sold a grand total of 51 razors and 168 blades that year.

Undaunted, Gillette changed his marketing strategy, actually giving away thousands of the razors to people. Once they tried his invention, he reasoned, they would immediately see its value — and he would make his real profit selling the disposable blades. This "razor and blades" business model, by the way, became one of the earliest modern examples of a loss leader.

It also boosted company sales the next year to 90,884 razors and 123,648 blades. For those of you doing the math at home, that's about 180,000 percent and 74,000 percent increase, respectively. Not too shabby.

Figuring that he was onto something, Gillette continued to offer the razors themselves for deeply discounted prices. A decade later, sales of his razor had reached 450,000 units, while blade sales soared past 70 million units.

Thanks to his "give a little to get a lot" strategy, Gillette's brand had become a household name and *the* market leader. And when the U.S. entered World War I in 1918, it was his company that was given the highly lucrative contract to provide each and every American soldier with a shaving kit. Gillette's strategy also paid off in the long run. Who can argue with the $57 billion the company was sold for to Procter & Gamble (based on closing NYSE prices on January 27, 2005)?

TRUST-BUILDING 101

Twelve of us sat around the table, several fidgeting with obvious impatience. This was the fifth meeting of our TEC associate group* and the same unasked question hung heavily in the air: what were we all doing here? Sure, we had met some interesting folks, but five months after joining the group, none of us had added any extra meat onto our business plates as a result of these meetings. How much more time were we prepared to give it?

As the TEC chair stood up to review the agenda and start the meeting, Brenda's patience finally snapped. "Ah, when exactly are we going to start to build the referral process into these meetings?" she asked with an irritated edge in her voice. Aha, I thought, this could get interesting.

The chair smiled, unruffled. "This *is* the process," he answered. "But I'm glad someone finally put the question on the

---

* TEC (now also branded as Vistage in several countries) is the self-described largest network of CEOs in the world. An associate group is a collection of business service providers that mirror the TEC CEO group in the diversity of services provided.

table —now we can really get down to business."

The fact is that all 12 of us were here for more than simply an opportunity to learn best practices, pick up some new ideas and profit from others' experiences. Deep in our sinister hearts was the real reason we joined: access to eleven potentially golden networks (and the CEO TEC group itself) we secretly hoped to mine for all they were worth. But months had passed and we had failed to realize the hoped-for business growth bonanza. More perplexing still was that the chair seemed to think this was entirely normal!

As I thought about it, though, I realized that he was right. Five sessions had given us time to get to know each other, to take stock of our diverse personalities, to achieve a level of comfort within the group. Now we were ready to move onto the next critical phase: building trust. Brenda's willingness to share her irritation rather than keep quiet was a sign — involuntary though it was — of that trust. And now that she had taken that step, it was as though some invisible barrier had fallen. We all began to speak out a little more openly, more honestly, sharing real information rather than platitudes. Our masks had come off, and we started to see each other as we really were.

Over the next few sessions, we engaged in deeper discussions about how we could accelerate the "trust" factor among ourselves. We also began to meet separately one-on-one or in small groups, speaking about personal issues and seeking each other out for help or advice in our respective areas of expertise. Most importantly, rather than worry about what we were getting, we began to focus on what we were giving to each other.

As I'm sure the TEC chair expected, referrals started to flow.

Interestingly, though, that has become less important to us than the kinship that has blossomed. In giving of ourselves, we have all gotten more than we expected. In the end, we all had to give before we could get.

SAMPLE-SIZE THAT, PLEASE

Whether it's attracting referrals or winning new customers, trust is absolutely the most important ingredient in the marketing process. The faster you can create trust in your product or service (or you, for that matter), the faster you'll grow your business. And just as the breakthrough in my TEC group happened when people bravely stepped out into the open with their real feelings, opinions and experiences, putting your business out there is the key to building trust.

Doing so inspires confidence! It says to prospective customers that you are so confident that they will love your product that you are even willing to part with some of it just to prove it to them. In marketing lingo, we call it "sampling," but I think such an innocuous little word doesn't appropriately convey the real power of the concept.

According to a survey conducted jointly a few years ago by Brand Marketing and the Promotion Marketing Association, 92 percent of those surveyed decided to buy a grocery, household or health and beauty care product after trying a sample. Nearly 75 percent said they had become aware of new or improved products through samples. And 84 percent reported that they would consider switching products if they liked the free sample.

We all like free stuff. More importantly, we respect the message it sends when a company offers us the chance to sample their product or service. If we like it, we're usually more than happy to pay — sometimes even a premium — for it.

My friend Michael Hepworth, author of *The Streetsmart Marketer,* is an advocate of giving a little to get a lot in return. "Are you a giver company or a taker?" he asks readers. "Companies are no different than people, and we are much more attracted to givers than we are to takers." Don't be afraid to give, whether it's free samples, free advice, free time or free information. Customers will appreciate the risk you're running, and if your product or service really is a good one, you'll earn their trust . . . and their (paying) business.

Besides providing samples, it's also generally a good idea to break up your service offering into smaller, bite-sized pieces. I learned that the hard way early in my consulting career trying to sell a comprehensive strategic planning tool. Although I'm obviously biased, I thought that it was a great tool, so I was understandably dismayed when a number of early prospects balked. Finally, a client told me point blank that he would be more comfortable initially with a stripped down $10,000 version instead of the deluxe $100,000 version. Although he said that he would probably spend the whole amount eventually (and he did), he just wasn't confident enough in the product to commit to such a large sum right off the bat.

I had inadvertently created a barrier to entry by insisting that clients devour the whole meal in one sitting instead of starting with an appetizer. Once I learned that lesson, I retooled the product and enjoyed considerably more sales success. After all, haven't we all eaten more grazing at a party snack buffet than we would have otherwise? All those small bites add up, you know.

KEYS TO ACTION:

1. **Give a little to get a lot.** Use the concept of "sampling" your product or service to build trust with your customers.

2. **Reduce the customer's risk.** Customers are reluctant to spend money on something they're unsure about. Develop strategies to reassure them that their perceived risk is low: guarantees, warranties, trial periods, etc.

3. **Offer bite-sized variants.** Break your services or product offerings into smaller pieces that are easier (and less risky) for your customers to digest. Offering different levels of your product or service (deluxe, normal, light) can also help prospects overcome their inertia and self-select the best fit for their needs.

4. **Deliver "surprise" value.** Keep your customers on their toes and try not to repeat offerings. For maximum impact, find a way to make a product or service offering an event that they can't afford to miss out on.

5. **Reward key customers and influence-shapers with "free" advice and products.** Even if they don't result in immediate, direct business, these kinds of gestures can have a dramatic and long-lasting impact. They help promote positive word-of-mouth, customer loyalty, referrals and excellent publicity. Plus, altruism just feels good.

Playing "Studio 54"

The more selective you are, the more attractive you become.

Studio 54: the nightclub to end all nightclubs. Its name alone conjures up images of decadence, drugs and the glamour of New York — at least for folks now over 45.

Founded in 1977 by Steve Rubell and Ian Schrager, the "Studio" quickly became the place to be, a Manhattan hot spot where both the famous and the infamous could be seen dancing and partying at all hours of the night: Andy Warhol, Salvador Dali, Mick and Bianca Jagger, Bob Fosse, Sophia Loren, Robin Williams, to name just a few. Rubell's trademark was appearing outside the disco's entrance to handpick the lucky few who would be admitted to the inner sanctum.

New York doesn't lack for swanky nightclubs, obviously, so what was Studio 54's tremendous appeal? In a word, exclusivity. Rubell was a master of the psychology of desire and ruthless in exercising its power. The more he refused entry to the hopefuls standing in line outside the club, the more intensely they wanted to get in, often waiting for hours night after night. For every person who was admitted, dozens were left in the cold — and the legend of Studio 54 grew.

Once in, patrons were confronted by an even more intricate series of "levels of inclusion." Each was progressively more exclusive; the innermost circle allowed partygoers to mingle with A-list celebs and Rubell himself. The greater the pleasure, the fewer who would be allowed to sample it.

In the end, Rubell was done in by his own hedonism, but that shouldn't obscure his marketing accomplishments. There's no doubt that he knew how to throw a helluva party, but his real genius lay in understanding how to create demand by limiting supply.

STRATEGY OF REJECTION

Playing hard to get has long been a tried and true strategy in the field of romance. Show your interest openly, so the thinking goes, and it won't be returned. Feign disinterest, though, and suddenly the object of your affection can't get enough of your company. (I'll be the first to confess that I've never been very good at it, though — my cool never lasted long enough to create the desired effect in my crush.)

Studio 54's growth plan capitalized on that basic psychological principle, creating an exclusive group of flagship clientele through a "strategy of rejection." If you invest initially in developing your customer base, it too can become a very strong marketing asset down the road as customers jostle each other to join your ranks. The adage that "you're known by the company you keep" is as true in sales as it is in society. If prospects see a top tier customer base, that in itself acts as a powerful third party reference.

Of course, that can be easier said than done, especially in the early going. I know (from experience) that when you start with nothing but bills, the thought of passing up any customer doesn't sit well. But in some cases, believe it or not, that's exactly what you must do. Too often young companies (especially SMEs) end up with customers they discover later they'd be better off without, customers who demand price concessions, drive up service costs and drain company resources. Other prospects see that and adjust their expectations accordingly, devaluing your brand . . . sometimes irreparably. The solution is a laser focus on the right customer and the right pricing right from the start.

SALES CHUTZPAH

One services firm I know — let's call it "Mango" — was founded on that principle, and its founders had the self-discipline, even in the face of mounting debt, to stick to it. They were careful to choose their industry targets based not only on potential business size, but also on the reputation the customer had acquired in the market. They knew that landing even a couple of these kind of accounts would invariably open other doors.

Once targeted, they conducted extensive research in order to understand the target company's operation and any "pressure points" relative to problems the company might be experiencing. That ensured that, right from the start, Mango's people knew more about the target company and its issues than other potential suppliers. They used a "warm contact" to get in the door, then cleverly even used some of the target company's internal lingo in their credentials pitch.

So far, so good. But this is where Mango's real chutzpah showed itself.

After the credentials presentation, Mango's sales people began to gently but consciously conduct their own interview of the targeted customer. They even went so far as to lay out Mango's own criteria for choosing the customers with whom it would work.

Role reversal! They pulled a "Studio 54."

It was pretty gutsy for a young and unproven company to

brazenly tell prospects that it would only work with selected clients, to in essence say "We choose you; you don't choose us."

But it worked! Time and again, the strategy paid off. Thanks to the founders' philosophy, Mango soon acquired a reputation as the new "hot" company everyone wanted to hire. Firmly in the driver's seat, Mango has achieved a quarterly growth rate of 40 percent or more for the past five years. As a post-script to this story, Mango was recently sold to a large multinational. Consistent with their business philosophy, the principals drove an incredible price for themselves and the company with their "you can't have us" strategy.

Mango's success is a primer on how premium brands become premium brands. Mercedes, Porsche, DeBeers, Rolex, Four Seasons — they all share the same game plan. "You can't have me," they tell all but a few exclusive few, "but don't you want me?" They set the bar exceedingly high, but there's still no shortage of customers willing to jump over it.

Funny thing, reverse psychology — in sales or in love. But it works!

KEYS TO ACTION:

1. **Start with a real point of difference.** Style is fine, but substance still matters; you can only so far on perceived exclusivity. Your product has to be unique in a way that goes beyond just image.

2. **Target your customers.** Build a system for choosing your customers and educate your entire organization about its function. Then research. Don't even

approach prospects until you fully understand them and their potential needs. Your objective should be to wow them in your first meeting with the strength of your knowledge — ideally, it should seem like you know them better than they do themselves. Use all legal means (and contacts) to acquire that knowledge: white papers, industry experts, the web, personal experience. Become a detective. The more you learn, the closer you'll be to getting their business.

3. **Start with a warm contact.** Network with everyone you know, asking them for recommendations about others who have a contact within the company or industry. Starting with this kind of personal recommendation lowers barriers and increases customer receptivity.

4. **Once in the door, tactfully let them know that you have "customer criteria," too.** Lay out your criteria and the rationale for them. Be firm! If in doubt, raise — don't lower — the bar. Your criteria should ideally inspire the prospect to want to be included in the group you describe, so make that group seem attractive and exclusive: industry leaders, companies on the cutting edge of technology, etc.

5. **Make it clear that you have very limited capacity for new customers . . . even if your dance card is really empty.** Regardless of how much work you actually

have in the hopper, give them the impression that you are incredibly busy, but you might possibly be able to accommodate the prospect.

6. **Price in nosebleed territory.** You can always relax a little on price for the "right" reasons, but you can never price up once the expectation is framed. Most of us equate price with quality: the higher the price, the better the quality. I liken it to a wine purchase. How many of us have the guts to serve up a $5.00 bottle when visiting friends for dinner? When in doubt, go higher. And above all, stick to your guns. Flinch even a little and it's "game over."

Price Is a Four-Letter Word

For virtually all companies, competing on price hurts more than it helps.

On the surface, Jetsgo was every bit the entrepreneurial success story. The upstart Canadian airline had lured customers away from the big boy on the block Air Canada thanks to an emphasis on discount fares. Founded in 2002, Jetsgo had become Canada's third largest carrier in less than three years, capturing 10 percent of the Canadian domestic market. With 19 destinations in Canada, 10 in the U.S. and 12 charter flights to the Caribbean on the weekend, Jetsgo seemed poised to be an industry player for years to come.

And then, in March 2005, Jetsgo simply . . . vanished. Thousands of travelers were left scrambling for alternate transportation when the company abruptly ceased operations during the height of spring break. Angry customer and industry pundits alike wondered, "What happened?"

Price happened. Jetsgo had burst onto the scene thanks to bargain basement fares, but ultimately its unsustainably low prices killed the airline. Company execs had hoped increased volume would offset the cost of keeping prices so low, but it never happened. And since the entire company's identity was predicated on offering the lowest prices in the industry, there was no way out of the trap.

Eventually there simply wasn't enough money to keep its planes flying.

RESIST THE URGE TO DISCOUNT

Pricing is the most difficult decision for any business, regardless of size. And virtually every company wrestles with the temptation to lure consumers from competitors and create market differentiation with low prices. Unfortunately, very few businesses can sustain a low price strategy focus over time. The sands of the marketplace are always shifting: competitors become more efficient, new technologies affect production, consumers' expectations change. And occasionally a company like Jetsgo rolls out a completely incompetent pricing strategy that hurts everyone in the industry.

Low price can be a valid strategy for companies that have invented a new way to go to market (Dell's direct buying model) or for those with business systems expressly designed to sustain this revenue strategy over the long term (Wal-Mart's focus on efficient replenishment and superior cost reduction systems). In both these cases, however, pricing was a result, not a premise.

And that's the secret: your ability to price either up or down is the ultimate measure of the effectiveness of your business strategy, not the foundation of it. Wal-Mart and Dell focused first on more efficient operations, which in turn has allowed them to be profitable at a lower price point than their competitors. Even for them, though, that's an elusive advantage. Ultimately, businesses that emphasize low pricing must maintain superior cost dynamics over the long haul; for those companies, cost reduction usually becomes the single overriding focus.

Despite the rarity of successfully competing on price, most businesses still attempt to use pricing as a differentiator. Don't! The last thing you should focus on is price — precisely because so many others do so. Instead, focus on building value for your customers and creating real differentiation for your product or services, which will allow you to support a price premium. Your real objective should be to support the highest price possible, not the lowest.

SLIPPERY SLOPE

The insidious nature of price discounting is that it usually seems to work in the short term. Price down and volume generally does go up. But appearances can be deceiving. There are two reasons why discounting ultimately almost always costs more than it's worth.

The first reason is that it usually attracts the type of customer you could well do without: the price "cherry pickers." These are the 10 percent or so of any market that are single-mindedly focused on getting the cheapest price. They are price loyal, not brand loyal, which means that they'll bolt the second they see a better price. They don't care one bit about whatever value-add you provide — and they definitely won't pay for it. Too often I've seen companies spend an inordinate sum to retain these cheapskates, only to get burned when someone else rolls out an inexpensive knock-off.

The second reason that pricing is insidious is that it can undermine your differentiation and actually reduce your ability to fund value-adding activity. By using discounting you are, in effect, teaching your customers to buy on price. Over time, they develop a "resistance" — they need increasingly higher discounts to motivate them to buy at their previous levels. It's a slippery slope, and the effort required to pull back is very, very difficult.

Here's an industry example of that phenomenon, with the names changed to protect the innocent. A company — let's call it Company X — was enjoying moderate success. Volume and profit were good, but share growth was languishing. The leadership team determined that they needed to accelerate their top line in order to demonstrate to the market that they had answered the competitive call and turned the corner. As so often happens in these cases, they chose the most expedient way to boost volume: price discounting.

To "fund" the discount, Company X instituted a one-year reduction in marketing and advertising expenditure. It wasn't a big cut, mind you, just a simple five percent reduction. But they had planted their corporate feet on the discounting slope.

The next year, the company budgeted a return to its previous spending, split between marketing and discounting. To the leadership's dismay, volume growth during the front half of the year declined. They shouldn't have been surprised; they were comparing the current volume against a time period in which volume had been artificially inflated by discounting. But since they couldn't afford to miss plan, they further reduced value-added spending (in the form of advertising and marketing) in favor of lower pricing initiatives during the back half of the year. Year two was more of the same, and when the dust had cleared they had spent even more on price discounting. The slide had begun.

Within five years, the company gone from spending 15 percent of its revenue on price discounting to over 26 percent. Despite this increase and the sacrifices it entailed (marketing support and innovation was slashed to fund the difference), Company X's market share had actually declined! Moreover, consumer research showed that the "quality" of the company's customer base was also lower than it had been five years earlier.

In the end, Company X was saved from utter disaster only through the actions of a new CEO who understood that in pursuing a discounting strategy, the company had mortgaged its future. He shifted the focus back to investment in real, sustainable top line growth through product innovation and customer-focused value. Slowly, painfully, the company pulled itself back from the brink and put itself back on course for long-term financial success.

CV = Q/P

Up to this point, our pricing discussion has focused on larger businesses. But for small and medium-sized companies, pricing is an even more difficult decision. The stakes are if anything even higher, and SME owners often feel tremendous pressure from their customers to deliver lower prices or lose their business. With lower reserves and ability to sustain even short-term loss, this may mean the difference between survival and bankruptcy.

Desperation drives these owners — desperation rooted in the fact that most of them have not developed a differentiated and sustainable position. Pricing, they too often think, is the only tool they've got.

But you must avoid the price trap. Instead, focus on building value by increasing service or product quality. If you ever find it necessary to reduce price to maintain your market position, it's a warning sign that your business is losing its value and isn't well-positioned for long-term sustainability. Unless you correct the "value problem," chances are that you won't be around too much longer.

The relationship between value and price can be best represented in a very simple equation: $CV = Q/P$. In English, that means *Customer Value* is equal to *Quality* divided by Price. Raise the price relative to quality and you lower the customer value; they're getting less by paying more. To increase value, either raise quality faster than price or lower price relative to quality (or both). Who said building value was tough?

One last point about how to price, especially for a smaller business: it's not always easy to determine the right price. On the one hand, a quick agreement with a customer on price leaves you wondering about how much money you inadvertently may have left on the table. Could you have priced higher? On the other hand, pricing too high can jeopardize business.

I always found this a difficult question to answer for my clients until I stumbled across the concept of value pricing. Simply put, value pricing is estimating the potential revenue and profit impact that your product or service could have on your customer and setting your price accordingly. The more impact you have, the higher you should price. Don't be afraid or ashamed — the clients that are worth having will understand and pay the premium gladly. As for the rest, well, send those cherry pickers to the next orchard. You'll be glad you did.

KEYS TO ACTION:

1. **Focus your primary effort on the numerator of the customer value equation, $CV = Q/P$.** Building the quality of your offering is a more sustainable strategy in the long term. Only a few companies win by using price as the corporate differentiator.

2. **Price relative to customer value generated.** Pricing to perceived competition reduces, rather than builds, perceived value. Believe in your offering and charge for it. Test high before moving lower and build your initial price relative to what you believe it will do for your customer.

3. **Watch out for the telltale signs of value erosion.** If business is becoming more difficult to keep or acquire, it may well be that your value perception or perceived differentiation is sliding. Two actions are required. First, validate your in-market perception by getting out there and asking. Second, redouble your efforts to build and reinforce your value perception. Introduce new, customer-validated services or products, or remind your customers about the value of your current offerings.

4. **Consider price discounting at your peril.** The short-term benefits of discounting are virtually always accompanied by long-term pain. If you do feel compelled to compete on price, don't formulate a price discounting strategy unless there's a built-in exit plan. Always know how you're going to get out . . . before you get in.

Your Customers Are Lying

Customers tell you what you want to hear. Look to their behavior, not their words, to guide your actions.

A few years ago, a well-known fast food company changed the oil it used to fry its french fries. It did so not because french fry sales had dropped or because there was anything wrong with the recipe. On the contrary, sales were strong and consumers consistently graded the fries very well in taste tests with competitors' fries.

But in that consumer research, the company also heard from its customers that they were concerned about health issues, particularly the fries' high fat content. What if, they were asked, the fries contained little or no trans-fat? The research participants responded enthusiastically.

So the company executives, seeing an opportunity to capitalize on this health-consciousness, decided to make the switch. They were confident that their move would win the praise of health officials and the approval of customers — particularly parents — nationwide. They fully expected a dramatic rise in market share and profits.

As it turns out, they were half right. Health officials did laud the company for providing a healthier option, although some also pointed out that a side of fruit or steamed veggies would be healthier still. Customers, however, absolutely hated the switch, complaining that the new fries didn't taste as good. Kids in particular refused to eat them — and parents, not wanting to push the issue, simply opted to eat at one of the company's competitors.

Instead of the top-line boost the company expected, sales dipped alarmingly. Within a few months, the old recipe was back in place and the "healthy fries" experiment abandoned. The brand damage took significantly longer to repair, as kids again had to be wooed into giving the company another chance. And the lesson?

Apparently, despite extensive consumer-focused research, the company's customers had lied to it.

WHEN RESEARCH FALLS FLAT

I saw something similar happen several years ago while working for one of North America's largest food product companies. A newly-minted, wet-behind-the-ears junior exec excitedly gave us a presentation in which he revealed an epiphany he'd had while conducting customer research: health concerns and the drive to healthy food was a reservoir of untapped consumer potential! The product concepts focusing on healthy foods had dwarfed any research results to date. A major consumer shift was in the works (and, he wanted us to know, he had discovered it)!

Poor guy. He clearly thought this was going to be the defining moment in his career. I think he was already mentally planning how he was going to redecorate the CEO's office — given his insight, it would only be a matter of time, clearly, until his talent took him to the biggest corner office in the building. To give credit to my colleagues, there was scarcely a snicker as we broke the bad news to him: his consumers had lied to him, straight bald-faced lies about their interest in health. And he had fallen for it, like so many before him.

The truth of the matter was that this was a very familiar pattern in the consumer research game, and it was particularly true for this particular region of the country. Despite having a particular penchant for "bad" food choices from a purchase and behavioral standpoint (high-sugar, high-fat products significantly outsold any "health" designated products), these consumers also consistently rated the healthy concepts the highest in interest and propensity to buy. In short, they lied.

Why? Because the customers wanted to live up to what they viewed as the socially accepted norm. They'd learned from the media that they were supposed to live healthy and eat healthy, so they answered with they thought was the "right" answer. Though deep down they probably knew that they would never really buy these products, they didn't want to be judged as fat or ignorant or socially unenlightened. So they gave the answer they thought the researchers wanted to hear, the one they thought most others would give, instead of telling them the truth.

Self-deception also plays a role. Maybe some of these consumers wanted to believe that they would buy the health-conscious products, that they would start eating better and exercising and getting in shape. It's well known within the fitness industry, in fact, that the best time to advertise for gym or health club memberships is just after January 1, when "get in shape" tops the list of most people's New Year's resolutions. Sign 'em up now when they're easy pickings, and never mind that nearly all of them will be gone within a month. Ah, the best of intentions …

Nor does this kind of customer deception occur only in formal consumer research settings. A former client of mine, Stacey, related a time when her company responded to an RFP put out by one of its customers. She knew a half dozen other companies were in competition for the job, but she and her team had put themselves wholeheartedly into the proposal process. Following the presentation, she left encouraged by the client's response: "Stacey, we appreciate the time you put into this presentation. It's clear that you put a lot of work into it and it represents some good thought. We have a tough decision to make, as you know, and we'll get back to you in the near future with our decision."

Stacey should have read between the lines. Phrases like "some good thought," "we have a tough decision to make" and "near future" are code words for "thanks, but no thanks." True, the customer hadn't exactly lied to Stacey — but he hadn't given her the straight goods, either.

MISCOMMUNICATION MISCUES

It's human nature to avoid conflict. That's not a bad thing in itself; thankfully, there aren't many people out there who delight in delivering bad news or dashing the hopes of others. This is particularly true in face-to-face settings. Think of an interview situation with a particularly horrendous candidate. How many times have you told them the stark truth? Not many, I'll wager. Why not? Perhaps because you respected their feelings, if not their resumé. Perhaps because you didn't want to risk a nasty emotional scene. Much easier, isn't it, to simply thank them for their time and give them the "we'll let you know" line?

Great salespeople have a kind of sixth sense about whether they're going to make a sale very early in the process. They can see it in a prospect's body language, tone of voice and eye movement. It's all about nuance. But it's tough enough for all but the most practiced individuals to pick up those indications face to face. How much harder is it to try to get the truth though long-distance, essentially anonymous consumer research efforts?

There's another issue at work here as well. Often we may be asking the wrong question, or not communicating our intent clearly. If confusion gets its foot in the door at the beginning of the process, consumers may misinterpret our questions or, even worse, we may misinterpret their answers. Even insignificant errors can lead to huge mistakes.

In most cases, therefore, you must test your hypotheses against observed behavior. All our young food exec needed to do in the example cited earlier in this chapter was to check to see what was really being purchased and he would have spared himself a lot of boardroom embarrassment. People can say what they want, but it's what they actually do that matters.

Perhaps the most famous (clichéd, by this time) example of a consumer research screw-up was the New Coke fiasco. Coca-Cola had heavily invested in consumer research before making the move to the new soft drink formula. Unfortunately for Coke, what's important is not the size of the investment, but rather the type and tone of the questions posed and the range of the responses generated. But what researcher is going to ask, "Would you be in an uproar if we took the beloved product you grew up with and forced you to purchase something different, which taste tests say that you should like as much or better?" In the end, it was as much about feeling as it was product attributes.

Here are some other examples of notorious commercial failures:

- **Iceland:** This successful British supermarket chain

attempted to go up-market by stocking only organic private labels. It backfired after its core low-income customers simply couldn't afford to shop there anymore. (Do you think that those customers would have "owned up" to not being able to afford it during consumer research? Yeah, me neither.)

- **Sony Bookman:** This follow-up to the iconic Walkman and successful Discman was introduced in the early 90s. It was basically a Walkman for books and recipes that retailed for $400. (Isn't it easier just to buy a book for $20? Apparently Sony's customers thought so.)

- **Xelibri:** A cell phone brand launched by German electronics giant Siemens in 2003, this was essentially phone fashion. Xelibri hoped to convince customers to replace their phones often, just as they would change other clothing accessories like shoes, purses, belts, etc. (It failed, but I wouldn't be surprised if this one reappears in another form.)

- **Happy Family Midge:** This innovative doll featured a removable "pregnant" belly containing a tiny baby. Some people mistakenly decided the doll was from the teen fashion line of Barbies and was promoting teen sex. Although Mattel tried to make Midge "respectable" by putting an image of her husband on the packaging, the company eventually pulled the doll in the face of continued protests.

- **Schlitz:** In the early 1970s, the company's new president cited market research showing that most beer drinkers couldn't tell one beer from another and convinced the company to move to a cheaper brewing method. Unfortunately for his theory, customers did, in fact, come to believe that a beer that is made more cheaply must taste worse. The damage was done and the company was sold to the Stroh Brewing Company just three years later.

The bottom line is that what looks good on paper doesn't always perform as expected in the market. Customers vote with their feet and are influenced by a wide range of external and internal factors — certainly more than your research model could account for. It's not that research isn't useful. It is. But research has its limitations. Understand those limitations and learn to look beyond traditional research methodologies or else you too could see your new flagship product sink under a tidal wave of anger or run aground in a fog of customer apathy.

KEYS TO ACTION:

1. **Start with role-playing (heard that before?).** Regardless of the specific situation, "putting on your customer hat" helps. Divorce yourself from your current position and put yourself in your customer's position. Try to get inside their head. Be skeptical. Criticize. Start with a "green field" and wipe your memory banks clean of what you thought you knew about the situation so you can better see it through their eyes.

2. **Qualitative research should precede quantitative research.** In a situation that requires more formal customer research, begin with a broad and open-ended focus. Every research expert will tell you that there is downside to qualitative research in that it doesn't necessarily reflect the target group's opinions. It is, however, very valuable for generating first-line hypotheses and deeper insights into the customers' mindsets. One-on-ones, focus groups, ethnography (living "in" the customer experience and observing) are all more formal ways of trying to get into the customer's heads in an unfiltered way. Very often the best insights come from unexpected twists and turns within the research experience itself. It can't be scripted . . . which is exactly the real benefit.

3. **Do your homework in advance.** The best solutions come to those with fertile minds. Prior to every customer meeting, whether an RFP or a research situation, immerse yourself in as much information as you can find. Debrief those who have experienced a similar proposal process, talk to employees in a target company to find out the real issues they are facing or political landmines to avoid, and study the industry and your competitors for the business. Pull out all the stops to make sure your preparation is as thorough as can be.

4. **Test your process before going live.** You can't assume that you'll get the reaction you expect, whether you're sitting in front of a customer pitching an RFP or questioning a consumer about food preferences. Nor can you assume your process is effective. You've got to pre-test. In the case of a pitch, use somebody not associated with the process to critique you. For consumer testing, use a small group to run through the process to ensure it works the way you think it will work.

5. **Use other ears and eyes.** Broadening the group charged with reviewing the customer information or sitting with the customer will help increase the accuracy of their conclusions. In a customer presentation, for instance, it's tough to keep on the agenda and watch your audience at the same time, so assign someone else the task — the more, the merrier. The same goes for more formal consumer research.

6. **Test for understanding and rephrase.** This is just a good communication practice. Make sure what you said and what you thought you heard is what was actually intended. Stop and test for clarity at regular intervals.

Listen Like Your Life Depends On It

Great leaders ask more and tell less. They know it's not about how much you talk, but about how well you listen.

During the bad old days of the Cold War, arguably the most important people aboard the hundreds of nuclear submarines prowling deep beneath the surface of the world's oceans were the humble sonar operators. Surprisingly, they weren't officers; many didn't have college degrees. And yet, their role was absolutely essential to the mission of each of these vessels.

Their job was to listen.

The primary purpose of each of these subs was either to track enemy counterparts or to remain hidden from them. So it was the sonar operators' job to sit in front of their console, headphones on, and listen to the sonar sweeps, straining to hear the sounds of another sub's propellers through the weirdly echoing audio clutter — sounds no novice could ever have heard. But their skill and concentration potentially meant the difference between not only success and failure, but life and death itself.

They listened as if their lives depended on it . . . because they did.

LESSONS FROM AN EX-PRESIDENT

A few years ago, I had the opportunity to meet former U.S. President Bill Clinton. I'll be frank — the prospect didn't exactly thrill me, as I was no fan of the man. As I stood there, waiting my turn, I had plenty of time to study the ex-President. Impeccably groomed, with an easy grin and a casual confidence about him, he worked the room like the pro that he was. And I noticed that although he spent only a moment or two with each of the people he talked to, he had them eating out of the palm of his hand. One by one, they took on an almost palpable glow, basking in the warmth of his attention.

"What is this man doing to these people?" I wondered. "Are they insane? Don't they realize that he's working them?"

Then he stopped in front of me, looked me straight in the eye and said, "Hello, I'm Bill. What's your name, and what brought you here today?"

I say that he stopped. At the time, it felt more like the world itself stopped. The room and its occupants receded from my awareness as I stood there, transfixed by this man's presence. He repeated my name, and asked me a couple of quick questions . . . and I answered, opening up far more than I'd intended to. The rational part of my brain knew that I was just another schmo getting the same meet-and-greet treatment as everyone else in the room, but it didn't matter. He made me feel as though he had all the time in the world to hear what I was telling him, and that it was the most important information he'd hear that day.

And then he was gone, moving on to the next guy while I felt that damned glow. Like him or hate him, you gotta give him this: the man is a master at what he does.

Maybe you know someone with the same knack for connecting with people: a great teacher, a terrific boss, an inspirational coach. I've met a few in my life, and I've discovered that they all shared a common trait. They knew how to listen. And not just politely, or disinterestedly, or tolerantly, either. They knew how to make you the focus, asking questions, drawing you out and making you feel like your opinion really mattered.

The technical name for it is "active listening." We generally do a lot more "passive listening" in our lives, though — silently nodding, covertly scanning the room, thinking about last night's big game or, most often, thinking about what we're going to say next. It's not entirely our fault, though, since biology doesn't do us any favors in this arena. Did you know that we speak at a rate of 100-175 words per minute, but listen at a rate of 600-800 words per minute? You don't have to be a math whiz to see that our brains have considerable downtime in which to be distracted by something more interesting (usually ourselves).

Active listening takes discipline. You have to force yourself to concentrate on what the person talking to you is saying; you have to curb your impulse to offer your own insights (no matter how brilliant) or shift the spotlight back onto you. You have to avoid distractions. You have to learn to listen, in short, like your life depends on it.

I doubt you'll find many, if any, folks out there who won't admit the merits of active listening. No one is going to say that it's overrated or unnecessary. Everyone admires the skill of those, like Bill Clinton, Abraham Lincoln and Princess Diana, who excelled at it. But most of us suck at actually putting it in practice.

THE "OOH OOH" KID

My father was a great active listener. He had a knack for sitting quietly in business meetings, listening intently and asking pointed questions every so often. It was a trait that amused my mother, who was a born talker. "You may be able to fool everyone else, my dear," I remember her saying to him, "but I know that half the time, you don't have the answers either. But they all think you're brilliant! Why?"

The truth was that Dad, who was a really sharp guy, understood the power of active listening. While everyone else was jockeying to make their opinions heard (and impress their bosses), he sat quietly and turned the issue around and around in his head. Often he hit upon the solution — or the right question — while everyone else was still playing verbal one-upmanship games. Not surprisingly, he acquired one of those coveted "still waters run deep" reputations that eventually prompted others to actively seek out his advice . . . and all because he was smart enough *not* to offer it at every opportunity!

(Unfortunately for me, I took after Mom. I was the "ooh ooh" kid in school; you remember, the kid who always had his hand up to say something, waving it and making that little "ooh ooh" sound like some demented orangutan in order to attract the teacher's attention? Yup, that was me. And I have to fight that tendency every meeting, every phone call, every conversation, every day. So if you're not a "natural" active listener, cheer up.)

At its heart, active listening is about changing your orientation from "me" to "you." It's about what you know, not what I know. It's about asking questions, not stating opinions. It's about cultivating empathy, not expressing ego. And as a result, it's about seeing what others frequently don't. And that's why it's worth learning.

Rumor has it that Bill Gates monitors a lot of the internal Microsoft message boards, reading the often spirited exchanges on research and development issues, corporate strategy, and competitive technology. He rarely interjects, preferring instead to watch others make their case. Things can get heated, and management decisions are sometimes openly second-guessed. But rather than compel obedience to the company line, Gates stays mostly silent as the discussions play out.

He's not, however, disinterested. Occasionally, he'll ask a key question himself or challenge one of the participants on a certain point. And if he thinks they're right, he's not afraid to change Microsoft policy to match. Pretty cool, huh?

If only we could all more consistently throttle that inner "ooh ooh" kid and learn to really, really listen. Who knows how much better our careers would be? How much more profitable our companies would be? How much more satisfied our clients would be? How much happier our relationships would be?

The next time you feel that familiar urge to interrupt, remember wise old Mark Twain's maxim: "Better to remain silent and be thought a fool than to open your mouth and remove all doubt."

KEYS TO ACTION:

1. **Practicing the art of "focused listening" starts with a mental shift — from you to them.** Make the speaker the focal point. That means developing the mental discipline not to think about what emails you need to send or where you should get lunch. Give the speaker your undivided attention, making frequent eye contact and resisting the impulse to "covertly" glance around the room, at your watch, etc.

2. **Watch the speaker's body language, but remain neutral to their emotional state.** Focus instead on what they're saying. Actively ignore your first impression of the other person. Whether it's good or

bad, the fact is that you've got to convince yourself that what they're going to tell you is completely captivating. Now pick out what actually is and focus on that.

3. **Put a mental "force field" around what you know (or think you know) to prevent you from accessing your knowledge base.** Pretend that you're filling an empty glass with the information you're hearing.

4. **Try to spend at least 80 percent of your "talk time" asking open-ended questions or following up on the information they shared.** If you don't understand something they've said, ask them to clarify. Summarize their position and restate it to them.

5. **Express sincere appreciation for their willingness to share their knowledge with you.** Even if you don't agree with it, make it a point to thank them for their time and insight.

PART TWO

Organization Fog Lights

"Yours will become a learning organization — one way or another."

– Howard Hyde, TEC Speaker

Monkey Traps

Focus is everything. To succeed, you must let go of some good ideas.

My friend Michael Hepworth is one of those unforgettable characters, a Rhodesian who has spent time running around Africa in the military before emigrating to North America and building and selling a couple of businesses. He now runs a very successful company that helps SME owners improve business growth. We regularly get together over coffee to commiserate about the challenges we see our clients facing. On just such an occasion, as I was complaining about the difficulty in maintaining focus in today's frenetic marketplace, he told me this little parable from his homeland:

Monkey meat is considered a delicacy among certain tribes in Africa. Conventional hunting techniques are usually ineffective against monkeys, however, since the little critters are simply too quick, nimble and intelligent to be done in by spears or traditional traps. But one tribe in Zimbabwe developed an ingenious and very effective way to catch the monkeys.

The set-up is simple. They hollow out a small gourd and punch a small hole, just about the size of a monkey's hand, in the gourd's skin. Then they place a few peanuts inside the gourd and tie the gourd to a tree or a peg.

Monkeys are notoriously curious, so when one finds the gourd, it can't resist sticking its hand through the hole to see what's inside. It discovers the peanuts and grabs a handful . . . and finds that it cannot remove its fist from the gourd. Obviously, it could simply open its fist, withdraw its arm and scamper to safety, but monkeys are also notoriously greedy. Even when humans approach, a monkey refuses to relinquish any of the peanuts in its grasp. As a result, any monkey caught in one of these traps is, as Michael colorfully puts it, "done like dinner."

TRYING TO BE ALL THINGS TO ALL PEOPLE

Virtually every week, I see clients — and to be honest, myself — in danger of getting stuck in "monkey traps." In a world filled with so many distractions, identifying and maintaining focus on a single goal requires an almost superhuman effort. We tend to become dazzled by new ideas and bored by old ones; we tend to think that if one good idea is worthwhile, ten must be even better. How many times in making a sales pitch have you at least been tempted by the urge to throw a whole handful of ideas at a customer, hoping that one sticks?

The problem with handfuls of ideas is the same as handfuls of peanuts. Too much of a good thing can actually decrease the odds of success rather than increase them. Trying to provide all things to all people can cause you to miss out on the benefits of targeting a specific market and capturing it through real differentiation. As counterintuitive as it may seem, both for monkeys and for us, less is more.

Take, for example, the Canadian retailing giant Loblaws Companies. Founded way back in 1919 as a supermarket chain, it grew to become Canada's largest grocery retailer (and the third largest in North America) by 1947. But aggressive acquisitions and diversification (including Sayvette, a discount department store chain) had helped get the company in trouble by the early 70s. In 1972, Loblaws Chairman Galen Weston hired Richard

Currie and Dave Nichol to turn the troubled ship around.

The new management team immediately returned the focus to the company's core retail grocery business, renovating its aging stores, building its infrastructure and developing strategic new product lines. The first major grocery product line out of the gate was a groundbreaker: no-name generic products inspired by Carrefour (itself a grocery giant out of France). Introduced in 1978, they were a tremendous success. Nichol followed up in 1983 with a line of "premium private label" products, marketed under the "President's Choice" name. More than simply price brands, they were touted as being of equal or even higher quality than the major manufacturers' brands. Nichol was featured in a series of television advertising campaigns, becoming known as Canada's "connoisseur of fine food."

By 1984, the chain had increased sales by 72 percent while net earnings jumped by a whopping 225 percent. In 1989, the company introduced a new "green" brand of environmentally friendly products, again to widespread success. Loblaws was back on top of the grocery industry, and remained there unchallenged through the mid-90s.

In 1994, however, Wal-Mart entered the Canadian market. Fearful of competition, Loblaws decided to shift its focus from grocery to mixed merchandising — in order to better compete with the American retail giant, management said. As a result, Loblaws' stores grew in size and complexity, selling clothes, electronics and household goods in addition to groceries, and featuring pharmacies, wine departments, dry cleaning, banking, fitness centers, tobacconists, consumer schools and even doctors' offices. Consumers who had been drawn to Loblaws because of the food, food expertise and comfortable shopping experience were now faced with a bewildering multi-service smorgasbord.

More than a decade later, Loblaws is a struggling company. Its stock price has fallen 40 percent in the past few years, its profits have nosedived and it has endured yet another management shake-up as well as a flawed consolidation of its regional structure, logistics issues and slowing retail growth. And all this in the face of renewed grocery competition from Wal-Mart . . .

Would Loblaws have been better served to let go of some of those peanuts and build focus and equity in their core grocery business? In my opinion, absolutely. The company's success came as a result of that grocery focus, its fall from grace as a result of its broadened business evolution into what its vision statement terms the "increasing assortment of everyday non-food products." It had started as a purveyor of great food and food ideas and ended up as a mishmash of businesses. Customers no longer knew what the company stood for; the company had lost its relevance to them.

A post-script: Loblaws is now trying to refocus its vision and return to its grocery roots. Only time will tell if it can regain what it lost.

DECIDING WHAT NOT TO DO

Advertising is another classic monkey trap. Messaging becomes diluted by trying to say too much or promise too much — what we used to call "trying to solve world hunger." More customer benefits are added in the false belief that this will help attract business, when all it actually does is to confuse your customers about the business you are in or the problem you're trying to solve. A plurality of benefits and solutions doesn't help — it hinders.

As a fledgling marketer, I remember an excellent presentation by Reader's Digest showing examples of good, effective print advertising. A key part of that success was due to a focus on one and only one consumer benefit, regardless of the product or service category. In fact, most effective communication starts with focus. A particularly insightful "creative" once leaned over to me during a difficult advertising meeting and whispered, "Oh, give me the freedom of a tightly defined creative strategy!" I thought that this was particularly interesting coming from someone assigned the responsibility of bringing a brand promise to life by creating compelling advertising. This guy was asking for focus!

Often the toughest job is deciding not what *is* to be done, but what is *not*. Here's a short exercise that will prove my point. Visit two or three company websites and read the "what we do" section or its equivalent. The vast majority of companies that I have worked with, regardless of size, fill that page with everything that is even remotely within their corporate capability that they think a prospective customer might want. Good companies, however, are centered. They know what they do best and usually couch it in terms that convey value to their target audience.

Look at your own website. Are you projecting a focused image, or are you trying to be too many things to too many people? Most of us are afraid to forego what could be some lucrative business or surrender another compelling consumer benefit. But by not letting go, we get stuck. I had that particular lesson shoved in my face just after leaving the hallowed halls of big business.

I was having lunch with a business acquaintance. The lunch went well, and we shared stories about what each of us was doing and what was keeping us busy. My friend listened intently as I spoke of the boards I had been asked to join, the book I was writing, the different consulting assignments I had undertaken . . . the list went on, as did the lunch. But when we finally walked to the parking lot and were saying our goodbyes, my friend looked me right in the eye.

"Sounds like you're pretty busy with all that you've got going on," he said. "Now let me give you some advice. You need to focus. It seems like you're keeping yourself pretty busy with all that activity, and that's good. But I still don't know what you do. My advice: pick the one thing that you really want to do and stick with it. You'll get better business traction that way than what you're doing now."

Ouch. I immediately knew that he was right, though. I was having a lovely time flitting from project to project, keeping six balls in the air at once, but my friend's tough love approach forced me to see the monkey trap for what it was. I was — and still am — grateful for his candor. But the dirty little secret is that I still daily struggle to avoid getting caught in that trap — there are simply too many good ideas and good business opportunities not to tempt me.

Discipline is a learned behavior, however. The ability to focus can be strengthened. That's good news all of us who are often reluctant to let go of even one peanut in the gourd. We can learn how to narrow our vision when necessary, to concentrate on the key goals and ignore everything else. That focus brings clarity for all stakeholders, both internal and external. It helps efficiently and profitably align resources, execution and understanding. And it keeps you from becoming someone's dinner.

KEYS TO ACTION:

1. **Start with an inventory of what you are currently doing.** Whether business activities, communication efforts or other some other endeavor, create a list of your current projects or messages. Ask yourself whether you are focusing on one thing or building a laundry list.

2. **Force-rank your list.** Be ruthless in determining your top priority — and you can't have more than one. Loblaws was in the grocery business, but they deluded themselves into thinking they were in the "customer service" business (standing for everything and nothing).

3. **Get some outside-in perspective on your "one thing."** It's not enough to focus on one thing, of course — you have to be focused on the right thing. Some outside perspective will help you determine exactly what that is. Remember that it is ultimately your customers who will judge whether you have chosen wisely, so test your hypothesis with them before you bet your bottom dollar.

4. **Test your focus by creating an "elevator speech."** An elevator speech is a 30-second synopsis of who you

are and what you do. Creating one will not only help you fine-tune your company's positioning, it will also help you differentiate yourself from your competition. A good elevator speech is tougher to create than you might think; I recommend the format suggested by *Crossing the Chasm* author Geoffrey Moore:

- *For:* Identify your target customer.
- *Who*: Follow that with a statement of the need or opportunity.
- *The:* State the product or service name.
- *Is a:* State the product category.
- *That:* Offer a statement of the key benefit or the compelling reason to buy.
- *Unlike:* Identify the primary competitive alternatives.
- *Our product:* Finish with a short statement of primary differentiation.

5. **Track your performance with a regular "dip-stick" test.** Step back on a regular basis to ensure that your focus is being maintained. Constant vigilance is required. It's easy to get caught in a monkey trap if you aren't paying attention.

Playing Organizational Small Ball
Big swings often mean big strikeouts. To win, you must test and seed many ideas, promoting the goal of "on-base" performance.

When he retired from baseball in 1935, Babe Ruth held the record for home runs (714), including most home runs in a season (60). The first record endured for almost 40 years until Hank Aaron surpassed it in 1974; controversial slugger Barry Bonds eclipsed that cherished mark during the 2007 season. Ruth's second home run record was edged by fellow Yankee Roger Maris in 1961, then by another big hitter, Mark McGuire, in 1998. Bonds hit 73 in 2001, a record that has stood since.

Less well-known, however, is that Ruth also struck out a record-setting 1,330 times during his career. That mark has been passed over 60 times since, however, as major leaguers have increasingly emphasized power-hitting and "long ball" baseball. Trying for Ruth's best, many batters have only succeeded in eclipsing his worst. Swinging for the fences, it seems, carries a risk.

Ty Cobb, meanwhile, was baseball's greatest "small ball" player, a man as admired for his athletic skills as he was disliked for his odious personality. His game was all about awareness, patience and discipline. Rather than swing big, he took advantage of defensive miscues with bunts, line drives into gaps and excellent base running. Year after year, his safe but unspectacular play helped turn his teams into contenders. Crowds didn't cheer his hitting like they did Ruth, but no one could deny its effectiveness.

When the Hall of Fame inducted its first class in 1936, though, Cobb surprisingly received *more* votes than Ruth!

THE NEXT BIG THING? THE NEXT BIG DON'T

While developing a seminar for some of the country's top executives recently, I had the opportunity to research what business leaders saw as the most critical issue facing their companies. The answer, overwhelmingly, was growth. "How do we generate sustainable, organic growth," they wanted to know, "both in terms of employee skills and the company's bottom line?"

In today's high-pressure business environment, whether you're the leader of a billion dollar multinational or you can count your employees by looking in the mirror, there's a compulsion to achieve that growth by swinging for the fences. The big idea, the big deal, the big acquisition, the big client — those are the home-run caliber swings that are supposed to result in big success. "Think big," marketing gurus say. "Act big." So . . . does it work? Does this all or nothing strategy really result in the kind of "sustainable, organic growth" business leaders want?

Emphatically no. In fact, most organizations are almost always better off playing small ball, maximizing gains while minimizing risks. Like Aesop's tale of the tortoise and the hare, slow and steady usually wins the race. It ain't sexy, but it works. Worry less about home runs and more about simply getting on base, and chances are that your team will win the game. In fact, in his book on the subject, *Profitable Growth is Everyone's Business*, author Ram Charan blasts the idea that growth is achieved through big swings. Actually, he points out, that's probably the least effective way to effect positive change. History bears him out — companies who have taken the all-or-nothing approach have ended up with the "nothing" many, many more times than the "all." Patience isn't just a virtue; it's a wise business strategy, as hindsight shows time and time again.

Since there's so much pressure to play organizational long ball, from investors, from the media, from unrealistic self-imposed hype, companies repeatedly find themselves grasping for the "next big thing" to bail them out of a pattern of bad decisions. I bet you've experienced some of these favorite flavors of the month:

- *The cost-saving initiative:* "All hands on deck. We need to do more with less!"
- *The growth initiative:* "We need ideas . . . NOW!"
- *The people initiative:* "We need change around here. We don't have the right skills. So, starting today we're going to train you or fire you and bring in people who have the right stuff."

These kinds of grand ideas are often popular with the folks at the top, less so with the employees in the trenches charged with the time-consuming and frustrating task of actually implementing the sweeping changes. "Here we go again," sigh the collective mass of employees who have seen it all before.

Most often, all that these programs accomplish is *"employee turtling."* Rather than embrace the most recent big idea, people retreat into their cubicles, keep their heads down and wait for it to run its course. They assume (quite rightly in most cases) that this new initiative will be no different from the last half-dozen started with a bang and ended six weeks later with a whimper. In the meantime, the best strategy is to keep a low profile and fake it until things return to normal.

Obviously, these swing-for-the-fences ideas can negatively impact not only business performance, but company morale as well. Instead of energizing an organization into growth, often they stun it into hibernation.

LEARNING TO PLAY SMALL BALL

Charan argues that before lasting transformative change can occur, both the business and its employees have to be taught *how* to grow. Doing so requires a cultural shift, one that depends on getting employees to buy into the overall goal. As we saw earlier, that's usually not easy. People are cynical about new directions and new directives.

Part of the solution is teaching them how to play small ball, emphasizing on achieving — and rewarding — small successes. Getting the small wins teaches the employees that they *can* win. As a result, winning becomes infectious, creating the momentum needed for positive change. Organic growth becomes gradually, steadily ingrained.

Small ball is tough to play because of the pressure to get something big done right *now*. We've all felt the pressure — the business isn't performing up to expectations and your superiors or shareholders are screaming for action. Just fix it! Do something! Anything!

That's exactly the time *not* to swing big. Stifle the urge to panic and focus on setting up the kind of sustainable processes that produce real, measurable results. You may have to set up a short-term, off-strategy move to create the breathing room to get your organizational feet back under you.

I was faced with just a similar challenge when I was given the dubious task of leading a turnaround in a large coffee business years ago. The business was broken. It had begun a decade previously when a collection of acquisitions had been managed as an afterthought from an organizational standpoint. With neglect came a steady stream of problems, culminating in alienated customers, disaffected employees and a plummeting top line. Eventually it became so bad that the higher-ups in the parent company realized that without a quick fix they were going to have a PR disaster on their hands.

After a crash course in understanding the business from ground level, my team and I mapped out both a short-term and a long-term action plan. The specifics aren't really important, but what is important is that we decided to play small ball by acquiring some "non-strategic" business in the short term in order to buy us time to seed a variety of initiatives that would result in longer term growth. We didn't pin our hopes on a single big new product offering or some drastic re-branding effort; instead, we focused on a number of smaller ideas — some proven, some innovative — whose cumulative effect would hit our growth goals.

The employees, by the way, enthusiastically supported the strategy — they were sick and tired of the parade of failed big ideas that had been forced on them over the years by increasingly desperate management teams, and they were all in favor of a more common sense approach. And it worked! Within a year, a business that had been losing 15 percent of top line growth annually (and was under water in terms of profit) had achieved 40 percent growth and a significant profit. As more of our "seed" ideas took hold, the company settled into the upward growth trajectory that so many swing-for-the-fences turnaround ideas had failed to produce. Playing small ball works.

Small ball works . . . but it relies on patience and planning. If you don't have a plan for your business — and I'm continually shocked at how many don't — start working on one. Today. Even something as simple as a one page to-do list can act as a focal point for growth, especially in smaller organizations. In fact, the phone book-sized business plans created by large companies are so unwieldy as to be almost useless. Your plan doesn't have to be lengthy or complex, but it does have to *be*. (Check out the "Plan on a Page" chapter for more information.)

In the final analysis, remember that great small ball players get the same shot at the Hall of Fame as the home run sluggers. Sometimes they even get more votes . . .

KEYS TO ACTION:

1. **Start with a review of what exists, and resist the temptation to "go where no person has gone before."**
   Why re-create the wheel? Spend some time searching the collective memory banks of the organization. Chances are there is already a tremendous amount of intellectual capital that already exists — use it to fast-forward your progress. Start with the proven. Look at what success models there are within the organization, past or present, and try them on for size again. Too often an organization will tire of a successful idea before it's worn out. Squeeze existing ideas for what's left in them; there's usually something still there.

2. **Create an "idea bank."** Create an intellectual reservoir for both existing and new ideas. This will provide an ongoing source of new ideas from which to draw when the business requires some additional "watering." Segment the ideas into levels of complexity, risk and resource commitment. One system I have used successfully in the past breaks the ideas down this way:

- *Existing technology/existing business:* These are the closest-in ideas, representing the least risk — but also the least incremental benefit.

- *Existing technology/new business:* Leverages what you know, but not what you're currently doing. Examples would be new categories of business, customers or new channels.

- *New technology/existing business:* Deals with innovation to your core business. Risky because of the new technology, but tempered by the fact that you know the business.

- *New technology/new business:* These are the home run swings, entirely new and entailing the most risk — but also potentially the highest reward. Consider them very carefully and use them very selectively.

3. **Think of process innovation as well as product innovation.** Sometimes the most successful ideas are not *what* you provide but *how* you provide it. Look beyond product to business system as you innovate.

4. **Engage the organization in the process.** Create the expectation that each individual is required to input and to create. Too often employees have an expectation that the ephemeral "they" will figure it out. "They" must become "me" if your organization is to grow.

5. **Create visible celebrations around each win, no matter how small.** Small celebrations and recognition will teach employees that they can, should and will be recognized for being part of the solution. Creation of positive momentum usually starts with a series of small nudges, not a giant push.

Make It Personal

Organizations don't change — people do. Successful change comes from strategies and communication that address individuals, not groups.

Like him or hate him, you've got to marvel at Tony Robbins. A few years ago, I sat in a huge auditorium and let my gaze wander over the packed crowd assembled to hear him speak. They came in all colors, sizes and fashions, from manicured executives who looked like they'd just stepped out of the boardroom to folks that looked like they needed a warm meal and a hot shower.

I came as a Tony Robbins agnostic, an observer. Clearly, though, I was one of the few that had come to prove rather than approve. An expectant hush fell over the crowd as the lights dimmed. Suddenly Robbins bounded onto the stage, the embodiment of energy and enthusiasm. The crowd erupted in cheering and applause; people chanted his name like he was a rock star.

I stared at the adoring masses, trying to fathom the phenomenon I was witnessing. People were enthused even before he had opened his mouth. What the hell was going on? Why were people so energized? What was his secret?

Once he began to speak, it was clear. He had the same skill that all truly charismatic speakers, leaders and gurus have possessed since time began: he was able to put each member of his audience on center stage. He made it personal, convincing each of them that they could control their fate, that they were deserving, intelligent, special people and success was within their reach.

Now who doesn't want to believe that?

IT'S ALL ABOUT ME

Whether you're the captain of the ship or the guy cleaning the head, we all worry first and foremost about number one. "How does this affect me?" is the question that comes most easily to our minds when evaluating any new situation. That's just human nature — at our heart, we're almost all narcissists.

Think about the last time you sat in an audience and really enjoyed what the speaker was saying. Subject matter and technical proficiency aside, I'm willing to bet that your enjoyment stemmed from the *individual* connection you felt with the speaker. Great speakers — and great comedians, musicians and other performers — are masters at echoing your unspoken thoughts, creating a shared bond. "They get me," you almost instinctively think. "They understand."

One look at Tony Robbins' website reaffirms that lesson. It positively drips with "me-centricity." "Life on *Your* Terms" proclaims the home page headline on the home page. Subheads focus on *your* health, *your* relationships, *your* career. Define *your* vision! Unleash the power within *you*! It's hard not to get excited thinking about all these tools designed especially (it seems) for you.

So why don't we all use this same approach when dealing with others? Chiefly, I think, because that kind of worldview is pretty alien to our own "me-centric" ego. Our impulse is to put ourselves at the center of our universe, and it takes a conscious act of will to put someone else there, even temporarily.

But keep that in mind when you decide to unveil "our" new company vision. While you're trying to keep everyone focused on the big picture, the questions that are racing through their minds are things like:

- *"What does that mean to me?"*
- *"Will my job responsibilities change?"*
- *"Will I still have a job three months from now?"*
- *"How does this affect my chances for promotion?"*
- *"Does this mean more work?"*
- *"Will I still have time for my family?"*
- *"Can I get a raise?"*

Bottom line: "It's all about me." Start with this in mind and you'll be much more successful engaging your respective employees, teams and customers.

RULES OF ENGAGEMENT

A couple of years ago, our senior team was grappling with the need to make some fundamental changes in the direction of our company. Our markets were stagnating, former customers had become our fiercest competition, our costs were rapidly escalating and our ability to create new growth was diminishing as we spent more money to address our current issue. We needed real change, real fast.

Prior to making a major overhaul, we conducted focus groups with our customers, spent time interviewing each other's departments to understand how we affected each other's work, and spoke at length to each other about the need for dramatic change. We spent a significant amount of organizational time ripping ourselves apart and trying to determine how best to reinvent ourselves. And for all our effort, it soon became clear that we were simply spinning our collective wheels.

Sure, we had diligently and conscientiously attempted to

engage our all stakeholders. But we had violated one of the cardinal rules of the "School of Tony": we had tried to do so on an intellectual and collective level instead of an emotional and personal one. Whoops!

For instance, we spoke often of the "company vision." We referred to organizational goals, to benchmarks, to best practices for the business. Corporate speak, in short. Unfortunately, that allowed our employees to easily distance themselves from the exercise. They didn't care as much about the company as they did about their jobs, their responsibilities, their opportunities. The organization wasn't at the top of their list — hell, it probably didn't crack their top five.

Once we realized that fundamental point, we saw that the change we wanted to effect had to start with individuals and scale up, not the reverse. With that in mind, we spoke to people about their individual needs, their aspirations and their individual contributions. We jettisoned the "organizational" speak and started addressing each person, asking them to complete a personal inventory of accomplishments as well as listing their frustrations.

We also began to consider how to link individual accountability with overall performance. It is very easy for an employee at any level to feel distanced from the company performance. "I did a great job," they rationalize. "It was the others that didn't perform. Sales blew it. Marketing didn't come through. The advertising stunk." Finger pointing is pretty easy at the organizational level. Create individual accountability, however, and it becomes a lot tougher — and, in turn, your organization becomes more energized and productive.

KEYS TO ACTION:

1. **Start with a "Tony Robbins" state of mind.** It's really no different than what's required of good marketing: put your clients, whether internal or external, at the center. Convince them that you understand their concerns and are genuinely are putting their needs first. Tangibly demonstrate that understanding through the services you provide and the way you provide them. All communication should begin and end with *their* well-being in mind, not yours (Copernican-thinking).

2. **Be consistent with your messaging.** Anything in your messaging that even hints of self-interest will damage your credibility. Most of us are pretty cynical these days — we're always looking out for the catch in any deal. Imagine what would happen to Tony's message if he suddenly began talking to his audience about how he planned to spend all his speaking fees and book royalties. Think he'd have a few unsatisfied customers?

3. **Watch your language!** Keep it simple. Headline and steer clear of buzzwords. Provide context and a "big picture" perspective. The best messaging provides links and a framework people can easily understand. Be personal and personable. Emotion is a good thing; it makes communication real. Speak like you would to a friend.

4. **Help them own it, but let them live it.** They have to believe that they have some measure of control and input, that they are the impetus of change, not the victim of it. Change can be scary, so you must be relentlessly optimistic. Break down the wall of fear by helping them see the benefit and then empowering them to carry out the change. Great athletes envision themselves winning. You've got to help your people do the same.

5. **Be clear on individual expectations.** People need guideposts, and the clearer the better. Give them something to push against so they can either sign on or sign out.

King Of The Hill

Build it, better it . . . and then tear it down and do it all again. Maintaining market leadership demands a never-ending cycle of creative destruction.

Legend has it that long ago there was a king of the Greek city-state of Corinth named Sisyphus. In some ways he was a good ruler, promoting navigation and commerce, but he also acquired a reputation for deceit, greed and trickery. After running afoul of the god Zeus, he was sentenced to be chained up in the underworld for eternity, but he managed to turn the tables on Thanatos, the avatar of death, and escape.

On another occasion, he instructed his wife not to offer the customary sacrifice upon his death. Once in the underworld, he complained of her neglect, finally persuading Queen Persephone to allow him to return to the world of the living to convince his wife to do her duty. Once back in Corinth, though, he refused to return to Hades and had to be carried back by force.

For his effrontery, Sisyphus was condemned to eternally roll a large stone up a steep hill. Just before reaching the summit, the stone would roll back down and Sisyphus would have to begin all over again.

Over the years, Sisyphus has become a metaphor for any difficult, never-ending task. It's also an apt metaphor for any company aspiring to be the king of the hill in its industry — just when you think you've reached the pinnacle, it's time to start again. Market leadership is truly a Sisyphean task in which complacency equals failure.

COMPETITIVE JOLT

I was barely inside the door of my first employer when I was faced with a monumental strategic conundrum. Now that I've had over 30 years of wandering the business world, I've seen the same basic scenario play itself out a thousand times.

Our company had established a firm leadership position in our market with a well-known, long-lived and generally well-received product: coffee. The decision in front of us was whether or not to introduce new vacuum-packaged coffee bags in place of paper bags (this was a long time ago, remember). The new packaging claimed to deliver fresher coffee because it prevented the coffee grounds from coming into contact with the air.

Despite that advantage, our customer research (and we had spent a significant amount of time and money evaluating the new packaging) indicated that consumers didn't perceive the vacuum-packed bags as an improvement over the older, more established product and package. Sure, they were currently buying stale coffee, but they didn't care. The new packaging, it seemed, was guilty of a classic marketing faux pas: attempting to solve a problem our customers didn't think they had.

The key issue for the company was that the new packaging was substantially less profitable. In fact, by introducing it, we would be effectively cutting our own throats relative to our returns. Assuming no market increase — and since it was a relatively mature market, significant growth seemed unlikely — our profitability would likely be dramatically reduced. For once our finance wonks and our customer research guys were in agreement, and it seemed an open and shut case . . . or so we thought.

A major competitor from outside the region saw this package

as a point of difference and a leverage point from which to contest our leadership, however. With nothing to lose and everything to gain, they invested in the newer technology across their entire portfolio and drove into our market with very aggressive consumer advertising. They positioned themselves as experts, trashing the old packaging as inferior. Our customers had earlier told us that they saw no advantage in the vacuum-packing. That was when the option was presented via concept boards in a controlled environment. Once a "sell" was involved by competition, they changed their tune and flocked to the new product.

Our competitor took substantive market share from us and forced us to react. Not only did it turn out to be markedly more expensive for us to hurriedly convert to the new packaging instead of managing the pace of the change, but we also lost our leadership image with many of our consumers. The company has been playing catch-up since that point — an expensive lesson of why market leaders can't afford to rest on their laurels.

CREATIVE DESTRUCTION

Back in 1942, an economist named Joseph Schumpeter coined a new phrase, "Creative Destruction." The process he wrote about described the transformation of a market as new, more flexible and nimble competitors rewrote the prevailing rules of the game. Innovation could come in many forms: product, process, thought. New competition changed the market paradigm, ushering in a new age of growth while the old withered away.

There are many examples of companies previously thought of as unassailable that succumbed to new market forces. Kodak,

Xerox and now potentially even Wal-Mart are just a few examples. Unless companies are able to continually rejuvenate themselves as active participants in their own "creative destruction," they will be eventually supplanted by their competitors. (The same principle is true for today's business leaders as well — if you are not continually remaking yourself, you are most likely sliding back into the corporate netherworld.)

Business literature is filled with stories and theories about how to build and sustain a leadership position. The current "poster boy" company for continuous innovation is Apple. As Apple's products and ideas have flooded the market — the iMac, OS X, iTunes, the phenomenally successful iPod and the new iPhone, to name a few — a steady stream of articles and news stories have also touted the company's brilliance in being at the creative forefront of the computer industry. Forgotten are the years of listless performance tied either by fate or fact to Steve Job's disconnection with the company . . .

IBM is also often cited as a company that has successfully practiced creative destruction, transforming itself from a computing and information services juggernaut to a consulting giant under the leadership of Louis Gerstner, who became Chairman and CEO of IBM in 1993 following a career as a consultant with McKinsey, an 11-year stint with American Express and four years as Chairman and CEO of RJR Nabisco. The IBM that Gerstner encountered was in deep trouble, and even today few people knew how close it was to running out of cash when he took the helm.

As interesting as IBM's successful turnaround is, (and we'll get to that in a moment), the root cause of its near-death experience is perhaps even more instructive. By the early 90s, IBM had created its own eco-system, growing both remarkably egocentric and horribly bureaucratic in the process. In addition to being self-centered, it had also become a decentralized, inefficient mess. IBM had turned its back on its most important source of both innovation and profit: its customers.

Gerstner's first action was to focus on cost improvement. He cauterized the financial hemorrhage by removing significant headcount and tossing out habitual cash drains like OS/2. He concluded IBM's chief advantage was its scale, so he changed the company's focus from hardware to more complete offerings that included software and service as well. He next focused on building centralization and accountability, so that compensation reverted from division first to company. Finally, he refocused the company on its customers and a "total solutions" mindset. While the effects of Gerstner's changes are still percolating through IBM, thanks to the new refined purpose Big Blue is making headway.

The task of a market leader isn't hard to understand. It's just hard to do. It involves change, learning and often even discarding successful behaviors or strategies. And if you don't think that sounds difficult, just try this simple example.

Most of us have an established morning routine: coffee, shower, shampoo, shave, etc. We also tend to perform those tasks in the same order in each morning. So I challenge you to do one of those activities out of sequence tomorrow morning. Just one. I suspect that you'll find that even that one small modification felt a little uncomfortable.

Change isn't easy, particularly when things are going well. After all, it's *necessity* that is the "mother of invention" according to the old saying, not success, prosperity or comfort. For change to occur, the inertia of that complacency has to be broken. In my experience in advising CEOs and their leadership teams, I've seen firsthand that you must convince the client that they are about to step into — or are already standing in — a big pile of poop before they will engage your services. Very few, if any, clients feel they need help if their business seems to be cruising right along.

Whenever I feel that I've become complacent or fallen into a rut, I picture Bill Curry, one of the most unforgettable characters I've ever met. The last time I saw Bill was in a geriatric hospital. He was 93 at the time, but despite some of the ravages of time, he had the youthful countenance of someone 40 years younger. There was a gleam in his eye as he retold stories of the past and spun his dreams for the future. And that was Bill's difference — he was always listening intently and dreaming of possibilities. Fascinated by life, he was continually renewing his perceptions and actions. He was a constant whirlwind of activity. If he wasn't lecturing (after a very successful run as President of Moore Business Forms) at Wilfrid Laurier's Business School, he was working his hobby farm in Southern Ontario.

So, what does Bill Curry have to do with market leadership or creative destruction? Better than anyone else I know, he exemplifies the passion for continuous improvement and reinvention that must characterize market leaders. If you want to remain the leader, whether corporately or individually, you have to embrace that reality. Build it, then better it, then do it all over again — just like Sisyphus.

KEYS TO ACTION:

1. **Use regular "dip stick" checks using outside-in feedback to determine your market position.** The market sees things before you do. It's also able to place you and your offerings in a much broader context, using information you don't have to provide a clearer view.

2. **Get unfiltered feedback from your organization.** A recent study reported that, when describing the characteristics of an organization, over 85 percent of senior leadership were at odds with the view held by the company's rank and file. Tellingly, it was the employees' view that more accurately reflected the view of the market. Use that perspective as a "canary in the mine" to give you advance warning of impending issues.

3. **Build an innovation pipeline.** Make innovation an essential business process no different than your mainstream functions, complete with objectives and metrics. Innovation should be present in every business activity you perform, not just in the products you provide. It can even come from the way in which you interact with your customers, your suppliers and your employees. Remember, every process has the opportunity to create advantage.

4. **Create "long range sensors."** There are many ways to look beyond the current market reality: consultants,

futurists, new communities. The broader your perspective, the greater will be your ability to draw analogies and create innovation. You may also choose to designate specific individuals or groups to research and communicate this advance knowledge to the rest of the company. IBM, for instance, uses new techniques to canvas the power of their collective intellect via the net. You might consider a similar method adapted to your particular circumstance.

5. **Play devil's advocate and fix it *before* it's broken.** Role-play your competition, or imagine that you are charged with the responsibility of changing the rules of the game for your company or industry. Brainstorm possibilities that could create competitive upheaval — and then move to capture that opportunity. Like Sisyphus, those companies that aspire to market leadership are condemned to a never-ending task of creation, destruction and re-creation.

The Narcissus Syndrome

Self-love is the great hidden danger for any business. The bigger you are, the more likely that you have created your own eco-system...and left your customers out in the cold.

According to Greek myth, young Narcissus was the most handsome of men, the son (many said) of a god. Most who gazed upon him fell head over heels in love. Echo, a lovely nymph, was no exception. Shyly conversing with him, she summoned up enough courage to reveal herself. But when she stepped forward, arms open to embrace Narcissus, the young man started back, exclaiming, "Stay away! I would rather die than let you touch me!"

Heartbroken, Echo fled to the nearby caves where she pined for her lost love, her flesh gradually shrinking away and her bones changing into rocks. Eventually, there was nothing left of Echo but her mournful voice.

Narcissus, meanwhile, shunned the other nymphs as well. One day, a frustrated maiden prayed that Narcissus might know what it was to love and not have his affections returned. The goddess Artemis, who had been very fond of Echo, saw her chance and cursed the young man. While drinking from a crystal clear pool, he caught sight of his reflection and became entranced. Unable to touch it, he remained by the edge of the water, entreating his elusive love, sometimes daring to kiss the surface of the pool.

Seasons passed and the vigor, energy and perfection of form that had captured the heart of Echo faded. Finally, Narcissus died there, a victim of his own beauty.

CORPORATE BLINDERS

Companies, like people, can suffer from the Narcissus Syndrome. They can become infatuated with their own publicity, products, services, brand or methodologies. And, just like Narcissus, that kind of inward-focused obsession can lead to seriously negative consequences.

The Narcissus Syndrome affects large and small companies alike. Entrepreneurial ventures are particularly susceptible because they rely so heavily on the perceptions of the owner/founder. That person wields two big sticks: the experience acquired while building the company, and the ability to effectively squash dissenting opinion. If the owner is even the least bit autocratic, job security-conscious employees may choose discretion as the better part of valor and stay mum even when they don't agree with their boss's proposed course of action.

Even vocal employees may find themselves fighting an uphill battle, and too often project planning and execution are forced to fit the preconceived notions of the founder and senior leadership of the company. As a result, the company ends up working from a skewed set of preconceptions about the environment, its customers and its overall business plan.

Back in 1972, Larry Greiner's *Evolution and Revolution as Organizations Grow* cited exactly this type of pervasive threat to small companies. Most entrepreneurial organizations, sooner or later, hit a crisis of leadership. The founders, burdened by unwanted management responsibilities, long for the "good old days" and unconsciously stick their heads in the sand when confronted by new ideas and new marketplace realities. Most of the time, Greiner found, new management is required to shift the company's focus; the founders tend to stand firm to the old ways even in the midst of trouble.

Unfortunately, I've seen this tendency in action far too often. A few years ago, I had the opportunity to help a hot young marketing services company build a strategic plan. They already had an enviable customer base and a novel method of creating customer value. The founders themselves were extremely bright, energetic and imaginative people — the ideal archetypes of the successful entrepreneur.

For bright people, though, they sure did some stupid things. They dutifully went through the planning exercise I gave them in order to identify both corporate beauty marks and warts. Then, just as dutifully, they opted to ignore the results. I advised, I cajoled, I pleaded, but to no avail. The founders clung to their preconceived notions of business reality, even when their company paid the price for their stubbornness.

I think that's why I so often have a love/hate relationship with entrepreneurs. I love their energy, their commitment and their faith in their vision. I hate the fact that they don't listen! So often they've had to build their businesses in the face of incredible odds and intense criticism that they've learned to only trust *their* instincts. Because they had to believe in themselves when everyone else doubted them, they've become constitutionally unable listen to anyone else.

It's the Narcissus Syndrome in action.

SOOTHING SELF-SUFFICIENCY

Juriscape CEO Harrison Barnes (talking about lawyers but applicable elsewhere) hit on five characteristics of the narcissistic individual, which I've extended to capture the personality of companies afflicted by the Narcissus Syndrome:

1. They are generally preoccupied with fantasies of limitless brilliance, power and success. They envision their environment as one that makes them the center of others' attention.
2. They have an exaggerated sense of self-importance that is far from commensurate with their actual level of achievement.
3. They lack empathy and are unwilling or unable to identify with the needs or feelings of others.
4. They are envious of those around them who possess strength they don't have, and they believe that others are envious of them.
5. They require constant admiration and approval.

For larger companies, the Narcissus Syndrome is brought on by a number of factors. The most common culprit, though, is simply the sheer size of the business, which causes a company to unintentionally become more distanced from its customer base and more inwardly focused. "As soon as you start listening to me and talking about *my* needs rather than yours, you'll get my business back," complained a former customer of the big multinational corporation I was working for at the time — a common theme for consumers tired of dealing with the bureaucracy of big business.

Big companies are also afflicted to a greater degree by politics than their smaller counterparts. Often, nobody in these organizations wants to be the bearer of bad tidings because they really do shoot the messenger. If that's the case, then the tidings themselves often are swept under the rug until they attract a hapless new messenger — or until they simply can't be ignored because of some imminent crisis.

Companies have a hard time seeing themselves for what they are. I recently had occasion to reconnect with my corporate alma mater while conducting a study for a major business school. Ostensibly, I was reaching out to companies to determine their future needs relative to leadership in their respective organizations.

But I have to confess that I had an ulterior motive in contacting my old professional stomping ground. I was curious to see if they had broadened their focus to include an external perspective, something that had previously been tacitly discouraged. At the end of the 45-minute telephone interview, I remarked that not once had the interviewee spoken of the environment external to the company. Silence. In that void, I knew that nothing had changed, and that the Narcissus Syndrome had claimed another victim.

"It is the nature of these people and organizations to deny the reality of the other's (the advisor or external environment) world," wrote the University of Virginia's Richard Ruth in his essay, "Working With Problems of Narcissism in Entrepreneurial Organizations." "There is an active move to try and destroy the facts supporting an alternate view in service of a soothing return to a narcissistic self-sufficiency." And therein lies the danger!

KEYS TO ACTION:

1. **Create an outreach program.** The fundamental cause of the Narcissus Syndrome is an extreme internal focus. The solution is to reach out for a balanced,

"outside-in" view of the company (or individual). In many cases, giving a third-party group the responsibility for conducting a confidential 360-degree review offers a valuable and conflict-free course of action.

2. **Ensure that your outside-in advisors are respected and trusted.** For their feedback to have any value, it must be believed. Ensure that your group of advisors are respected and trusted *before* they review the situation and provide input.

3. **Take the "narcissists" out of their comfort zone.** When dealing with a situation in which the Narcissus Syndrome is deeply entrenched, you must weaken institutional self-defense mechanisms by challenging the belief system in advance. Subject experts in particular are a great way to introduce new ideas or knowledge into the mix and start the wheels of change moving. Be sure to keep the focus on the information itself and avoid personality clashes or political squabbling if at all possible. To that end, schedule events like company planning exercises in a neutral environment. Doing so will help move people away from any turf they feel compelled to defend.

4. **Use case studies that help reflect the current situation.** You can learn from your own mistakes, but it's usually preferable to learn from the mistakes of

others. Case studies can be very illustrative — and they have the added advantages of being both authoritative and non-confrontational. People are often more likely to draw the appropriate conclusions from other situations more readily than through self-analysis. Use case studies to "jog" the corporate brain.

5. **Be appropriately direct.** Sometimes tact works. Sometimes you've got to use a two by four to get folks to pay attention. If that's the case in your organization, be prepared to inject a little pain in order to get the gain.

The Hole in the Wall

The three sweetest words in business are "positive cash flow."

Driving to the grocery store a few years back, I turned to my wife and groused about how expensive everything was becoming. No matter how hard we tried, it seemed like I couldn't keep my wallet from leaking cash.

My litany of complaint was interrupted by a sweet little voice from the back seat: my four-year-old daughter. "Daddy?" she said. "You don't need to worry about money. If we need more, you can always get it from the hole in the wall."

Hole in the wall? It took me a minute to figure out that she was talking about the ATM machine outside our local bank branch, the one my wife and I used when we needed some quick cash. In her innocence, she assumed that the money was just there for the taking. Need cash? Just go to the hole in the wall. There's always lots there!

CASH FLOW IS KING

I'm tempted at times to tell that story to certain clients of mine, especially when they get thick-headed about cash flow issues. No matter how hard I hammer it home, some of them just don't seem to understand that there is no magical hole in the wall from which businesses can take money when they need it. To get cash out, you first have to have put cash in. Simply put, the difference between how much you put in and how much you take out is your cash flow. If the flow increases, that's good. If it decreases . . . well, you may be in for a rocky road.

I was stunned to find that cash flow is a fairly new requirement for financial reporting, a rule only since 1988. That surprises me, since its benefit to investors and management alike is obvious. Cash flow shows how much actual money the company is generating. Unlike other measurements and statements, like the P&L, there is little a company can do to manipulate its cash position. The cash flow statement, therefore, should be center stage as a measure of the business. Despite this fact, few businesspeople are as adept at creating and analyzing a cash flow statement as they are the P&L. For the sake of your company's health, though, you should be. Cash flow, remember, is king.

Time and again I encounter situations like the one that happened to an acquaintance of mine — we'll call her Jane. Smart, knowledgeable and polished, Jane had recruited a stellar advisory board for her fledgling start-up. At their first group meeting, she walked them through the fundamentals of her business concept and the assumptions that she'd made relative to market size and likely competition. Heads nodded in approval. So far, so good, she thought.

Then she began discussing the working capital requirements of the business. After describing the month-by-month projections, the room fell silent. Butterflies fluttered again in Jane's stomach as she waited for someone, *anyone*, to say something. Finally, a single hand went up.

"Jane, up until this point I've been very impressed with your presentation," said the man, a veteran of numerous start-up ventures. "It seems extremely well thought out. I do have a major issue, however, with the degree to which you've allowed yourself a safety zone relative to the amount of cash you think you will need in the second half of the year. In my experience, it's far better to borrow more than you think you need in the start-up phase to cover those unexpected, unlooked for events. Most of the start-ups I know failed because they lacked the available cash to continue running the business in the wake of those events. Better to be safe and spend a little more on creating that safety zone now than be sorry and have to scramble for a cash infusion later."

Unfortunately for Jane, she opted not to take her board's wise advice, and she paid for it, literally. Faced with a significant cash flow issue in the back half of her first year of operation, she had to give up almost half the equity in her new venture in order to parachute in the cash needed to keep the doors open. It was an expensive lesson about the importance of cash flow — and one that occurs all too frequently.

JUST SAY NO

I am continually amazed to discover just how few companies and executives really understand the concept of cash flow. Too often businesspeople (and entrepreneurs especially) confuse cash flow with profitability. But that's misleading, and it can lead to bad decisions and poor planning.

As I said earlier, cash flow reflects the net amount of cash (real expense and revenue) entering or leaving the business over any given time interval. It does not include *future* incoming and outgoing cash that has been recorded on credit. Net income (profit), on the other hand, does include sales on credit and other estimated items such as amortized depreciation. Positive cash flow means that the company is building the funds necessary to run and reinvest in the business. Negative cash flow means the company is being drained of its resources.

Elsewhere in this book, we talk about the importance of cash flow as it relates to valuing a business for purchase or sale. But it is also important to understand the cash requirements of your business. Just take the example of another acquaintance of mine, Peter.

Peter was a savvy entrepreneur who had in five years' time built his business into a substantial concern from the ground up. Then came the day that a very influential prospect decided to place an order than far exceeded the company's current capacity. On the one hand, if they pulled it off, the company might take that next critical step in both profitability and reputation. On the other hand, he'd heard plenty of horror stories of companies just like his going under from the weight of the business that they'd accepted.

Peter knew that the cash required to service the inventory build-up far exceeded his current line of credit with the bank. He'd have to mortgage everything just to make sure he could deliver the product. If anything went wrong, he'd be screwed.

A lot of agonizing soul searching later, Peter decided to decline the offer. He told the customer honestly that his business wasn't yet equipped to deal with the cash pressure that this order would create — it was just too risky.

To its credit, the customer rewarded Peter's honesty. "The fact that you recognized your situation makes you just the type of company we want to deal with," the purchasing agent told him. "Let's cut this order back to what you feel is comfortable this time around. We'll run the item in a limited distribution in our stores and see how it works out. We believe in win-wins. In time, you'll be better able to handle the size of the business we'll throw your way."

While you can't count on a customer being as understanding

as Peter's, you can avoid serious trouble by gritting your teeth, knowing your limitations and following his example. Unfortunately, in most of the stories I hear and see being played out, owners simply can't bring themselves to do that. As a result, of the reported nine of 10 business ideas that head south, I would venture to say that the majority do so because of cash flow issues. It is all too common to underestimate the amount of cash needed to sustain a business, so err on the side of caution.

KEYS TO ACTION:

Here are several things you can do to improve your cash flow:

1. **Price up.** That's often easier said than done, of course, especially when you're facing competitive pressure, declining volume or loss of customers. But there's no getting around the fact that bringing in more revenue is always a good thing for the business. You can also effectively price up across your business by changing the product mix to more aggressively promote higher margin items, for instance, or by moving to price on selective items or segments.

2. **Reduce input costs.** Retailers do this all the time, regularly holding "line reviews" that pit suppliers of similar items against each other in order to win "preferred" status within the stores. Whether it's formal or not, you should be regularly holding this type of review as well for all your ongoing costs. If you manufacture a product, this review should encompass not only the raw material needed but also

every expense associated with your business: insurance, travel, meeting, etc. There are also a myriad of companies out there that make their money by taking a piece of whatever cost reduction they find. Use them. You'll find that the risk is minimal and the payoff is potentially huge.

3. **Reduce your inventory.** Thar's money in them thar office supplies, pilgrim! Inventory exists at all levels of the business, even that one, and it costs you. That's why "just-in-time" supply management was developed — it transfers most of the inventory cost to your supplier, while you're supplied only when you need an item (products or merchandise, stationary, equipment) and not before. This drives down the amount of cash used to purchase and hold a "surge" protection of inventory, freeing up additional financial resources to grow the business.

4. **Shorten your receivables, lengthen your payables.** Remember General Patton's famous advice to his soldiers: "Your job is *not* to die for your country, it's to make some other poor bastard die for his"? Shortening your receivables and lengthening your payables is the business equivalent. If somebody is paying you faster, it means that they're laying out their cash quicker. Good for you, not so good for them. Meanwhile, taking more time to pay others allows you to keep your cash longer.

To help shorten receivables, try a carrot and stick approach. Experiment with a small discount for customers who pay early (the carrot), but impose a slightly stiffer penalty on those who pay late (the stick). Implement a good tracking process that not only considers the aging of receivables but also provides a trigger for collection.

5. **Smooth your expenses.** When it comes to equipment, office space, vehicles and such, should you buy or lease? Before making an assumption about which offers the most economic benefits for your company, take the time to study the issue. Will the interest payments or additional lease costs offset the cash flow benefits of smoothing?

WWMD
(What Would Machiavelli Do?)

Forget fads. Good management and values practices are timeless. Machiavelli was, and still is, bang on!

Historians have been generally unkind to Niccolo Machiavelli, the notorious Renaissance political philosopher. His name has become synonymous with cunning, deviousness and duplicity, conjuring up images of corrupt rulers who use an "ends justify the means" mentality to rationalize policies that prey on the weak.

The reality couldn't be more different. Born in 1469, Niccolo di Bernardo dei Machiavelli was actually an irreverent, often sardonic and widely-read intellectual who ardently championed the Florentine republic while possessing a broad streak of nostalgia for the old Roman Empire — because, ironically enough, he felt men dealt with each other more honorably and honestly in those days.

Machiavelli entered government service in 1494, the same year that Florence expelled the ruling Medici family and declared itself a republic. A keen observer of psychology, he was given a number of diplomatic missions before being appointed the commander of Florence's citizen militia in 1503, in which role he was responsible for the city's defense. In 1512, however, the Medici regained control of Florence. As a key figure of the republican government, Machiavelli was removed from office, imprisoned and tortured.

Upon his release, a wearied but wiser man, Machiavelli retired to his country estate and devoted himself to writing a number of political treatises dealing with obtaining and holding political power. His best known work, *The Prince*, was designed as a handbook for a young ruler struggling to consolidate his position in the face of external opposition and internal criticism.

It was, in a sense, history's first guide for managers — and five centuries later, it remains remarkably relevant, insightful and useful.

MACHIAVELLI'S ART OF THE DEAL

Although I first read *The Prince* in high school, it wasn't until years later that I came to really understand and appreciate its insights. I still remember the episode vividly. Our executive team was in the boardroom debating the pros and cons of acquiring a specific company. Its products would allow us to broaden our business scope, but it was well-known that this particular company was fiercely independent, having absorbed many of the entrepreneurial traits of its founder. (It had a unique personality!)

Our conversation centered on the "people side" of the integration post-acquisition. Would the two differing corporate cultures make integration exceptionally difficult? How critical was the other company's founder to the "magic sauce" that had kept his company successful? Were we about to bite off more than we could chew — or at least end up with a bad case of acquisition indigestion?

As I sat listening to the back-and-forth, something clicked in my mind and I remembered something Machiavelli wrote in *The Prince* about the difficulties of absorbing new territorial conquests. I reread the book after the meeting, and it has been a constant companion since that date. I've found that although Machiavelli was focused on city-states, the principles he outlines apply amazingly well to modern business organizations and the executives responsible for their performance. Consider, for example, some of his lessons concerning the types of City-states (today's companies) and how they should be managed or acquired:

There are only two fundamental types of organizations.

Organizations are either established or new. "New" can mean a young company, like a start-up, or a recent acquisition (a part of another organization that has been sold or a free-standing organization in its own right).

MACHIAVELLI ON ACQUISITIONS

It is easier to integrate previously owned organizations than new ones. Independent companies by nature have more deeply held values and processes, which makes change more difficult.

To keep things running on an even keel as the new owner of an acquired business, you must deal fairly with issues as they arise while refraining from trampling on the older company's values and processes. Barring any unfortunate faux pas in these areas, eventually the acquisition's collective memories will fade — and with them, any remaining dissent to the merger.

Acquiring another company comes at a cost that must be repaid. To recoup at least part of the expense, "synergies" are sought, usually coming in the form of substantive cuts in both programming and people in the acquired organization. In making these cuts, you can quickly made enemies of all those who have been hurt through the acquisition process and their allies. The best way to avoid this is to recognize the potential issues and execute the required actions quickly and with as much sensitivity as possible.

The more similar the nature of two merging companies, the easier the integration will be. The greater their differences, the more difficult the process of integration will be.

Machiavelli's advice in this regard boils down to two main tenets: "out with the old" and "walk a mile in their shoes." To obtain a firm hold on the new acquisition, the leadership of the acquired company should be let go. And the sooner the better. Doing so allows you to form new relationships ("new alliances") with the employees. That leads to the second part of the equation, allowing the employees to see and meet with representatives of the acquiring company. "He who has acquired them should go and reside there," said Machiavelli. "This would make his position more secure and durable." If that is impossible or impractical, at least send "emissaries" to the acquired organization to deal immediately with issues as they arise. The implications of this advice is clear: get involved with your new company and its employees as soon as possible. Be seen. Reside there and get the two employee bases interacting with each other as soon as possible.

It is easier to acquire and hold an independent stand-alone company than one composed of several separate units or divisions.

In an independent company, leadership is likely to be consolidated in the form of a President and a group of functional leads who rely on the President's favor to continue in their position. A conglomerate, on the other hand, usually possesses a more diversified leadership structure. Machiavelli points out that although it may be difficult to assume control of the first situation, once having done so, that control is more easily retained — one master replaces the former one. Conglomerates or companies with strong divisional structures may be comparatively easy to "win over," since there are always malcontents in positions of power that desire change. Once in your possession, though, you may face difficulties in dealing not only with those who resisted you, but even with those who assisted in the acquisition. Why? Simply stated, since leadership was widely held, there are a lot of egos out there. Not all of them are going to be happy with the changes, and odds are at least some of them will take the opportunity to express their displeasure in some way.

There are three options for handling the leadership of self-governing organizations after an acquisition: get rid of the leaders, become a part of the organization yourself, or allow the leaders to remain as long as they demonstrate their loyalty to the new order.

Frankly, Machiavelli's strongest advice is to — figuratively, anyway — cut off the old leader's head. Since an organization used to the rule of a traditional hierarchical structure is accustomed to obey orders, eliminating the "old regime" removes the prime source of potential rebellion. With no clear line of internal succession, the likelihood of organized discontent is reduced and the organization's natural habits should soon reassert themselves with you at the top.

MACHIAVELLI ON LEADERSHIP

Machiavelli wrote extensively about acqui . . . uh, conquest, but he was also concerned with the nature — and ethics — of leadership. How should a successful prince behave? How important is it that he be liked? Respected? How does he go about managing change? Do the ends really justify the means?

A small sampling of his advice emphasizes the need for prudence, experience and decisiveness.

Successful organizational change is tough stuff.

"There is nothing more difficult or more perilous to conduct, or more uncertain in its process than to take the lead in the introduction of a new order of things," Machiavelli wrote. Why? Invariably, the instigator of change creates enemies in those who have done well in the previous model while winning only lukewarm defenders in those who may do well under the new. Successful change, he argues, comes about through a combination of both "force and ability." In other words, organizational inertia will thwart anyone who lacks the authority to compel change, no matter how good their ideas may be. Successful initiatives must be top-down driven, not arise in the "middle" of the organization.

Luck only gets you so far — there's just no substitute for experience.

Machiavelli points out that those who have reached the top of an organization through good fortune are usually destined to fail. Because they haven't been put through the wringer, their experience base is insufficient and when put to the test they're likely to fall short. Good leadership requires a firm foundation on which to build. If not laid at the outset, it is very difficult to do so later. There's no substitute for experience.

Live by the sword, die by the sword.

While history shows that it is possible for "villains" to acquire positions of leadership through deceitful or duplicitous means, it also shows that they usually get what's coming to them. Such methods may gain empire but not glory, he says, and the gains achieved through guile and falsehood will eventually fall away. If you are intent upon this ignoble course, however, he advises that you make your deceit an isolated event — one bad act can be explained away, but a pattern of behavior cannot be ignored.

Use your head, don't lose it.

You can't be both a leader and one of the people. That means hard decisions, but it's better to be respected than loved. And while a wise leader seeks advice, ultimately it's the leader's call — leaders lead. Sometimes that involves choosing the lesser of two evils. Deal with it. It may also involve breaking a promise when the original circumstances change. While Machiavelli doesn't advocate going back on your word frivolously, he also says that keeping a promise you know will produce a bad result isn't smart, either. If you do have to change your mind, communicate to the affected parties why the promise can't be kept (unless the need for confidentiality demands otherwise).

Good, practical principles for good, effective leadership. Machiavelli's name has been so tarnished by posterity that you may never win friends by publicly declaring yourself a fan. But keep a copy of *The Prince* in your desk drawer nevertheless, and make it a point to consult it frequently. You won't regret it — I know I haven't.

KEYS TO ACTION:

1. **Determine your current situation relative to Machiavelli's organizational model.** Are you a new organization or an established one? Are you about to acquire someone?

2. **Ask yourself, "WWMD: What would Machiavelli do?"** Look at your contemplated future actions and compare them to Machiavelli's advice. What changes – if any – should you make to your plan or organization? Use Machiavelli's organizational philosophy as a guide when considering your organization and future action.

3. **Write it down.** Use your existing template or, even better, the plan on a page model articulated at the end of this section of the book, to encapsulate your thoughts.

4. **Engage your leadership.** Communicate the rationale for and benefits of your vision. Solicit input from key stakeholders.

5. **Read (or re-read)** *The Prince.* Get a copy you don't mind marking up, and make notes in the margins. I guarantee that you'll find a great many pearls of wisdom. For more insights into Machiavelli's complex character, find a copy of Sebastian de Grazia's Pulitzer Prize-winning biography, *Machiavelli in Hell.*

How To Build A Leprechaun Trap
To reap the pot of gold, you must plan your business exit strategy as diligently as you have built your business.

Once upon a time, a farmer was out walking in his field. The day was beautiful and full of promise, and the farmer was very pleased with the progress of his crop. Suddenly he heard some kind of scratching noise just beyond a small knoll. Concerned that a gopher might have invaded his field, the farmer went to investigate. As quietly as he could, he snuck over the rise to see for himself.

Imagine his surprise when he saw not the gopher he feared, but a small figure in a green suit: a leprechaun! The leprechaun was so intent digging a hole that he was unaware of the farmer's approach until the man suddenly grabbed him from behind.

"You're a leprechaun," the farmer said accusingly.

"Aye," the little creature confirmed a little sourly, "I am indeed."

"Well, then, where's your pot of gold? In every leprechaun story I've ever heard, the leprechaun has a pot of gold."

"'Tis buried in this field deep beneath another plant," said the leprechaun. "If you promise not to hurt me, I shall tell you where."

The farmer agreed, and the leprechaun pointed to the plant. The farmer took a piece of red string from his pocket and tied it around the stem of the plant. "If I release you, you must promise me not to remove this string," he said. The leprechaun, scowling, agreed.

The farmer hurried back to his barn to fetch a shovel,

congratulating himself on his cleverness. He thought of all the uses for the gold that would soon be his: a big new farmhouse, a prize-winning milk cow, perhaps an orchard. Soon he would be the most important man in the whole village . . .

Within 20 minutes he was back at the spot where he had captured the leprechaun. The shovel fell from his suddenly nerveless hand and his mouth fell open as he gazed out on his field — each plant sported an identical red string tied around its stem.

Score another one for the leprechaun.

BUILDING YOUR TRAP IN ADVANCE

Many of the business owners I've known throughout the years must have been cut from the same cloth as our friend the farmer. They seem to believe that there's a pot of gold waiting for them under their business as well, just waiting to be unearthed when they finally put their company up for sale. They've worked hard to build the business, after all; why wouldn't it fetch a pretty penny from some prospective buyer?

Most of them, unfortunately, are in for the farmer's rude awakening. Perhaps the moment of disillusionment occurs when they engage a broker to value their business and discover that it's not worth nearly as much as they thought. Perhaps it's when a second opinion only confirms the first, or when the business sits on the block for month after interminable month, attracting little buyer interest. Or perhaps it's when they finally knuckle under and either accept an amount far less than that required to finance the lifestyle they had dreamed about or accept that they're in this for the long haul.

What these unfortunates discover only too late is the reality that if you want to catch a leprechaun, you'd best build your leprechaun trap well in advance. Translation: expend as much effort planning your exit strategy as you have in building the business itself.

Sometimes people get it right. One of my acquaintances, Mary, had started a business in her basement selling her homemade salad dressings, which all her friends had raved about for years. Slowly the business grew, moving from the basement to the garage, as she added customers and new flavors. A few years in, John joined the business as a partner, and with his help the brand made inroads into most of the major retail grocery chains. Ten years after Mary first decided to take the plunge, her company had weathered the early growing pains and seemed to be looking at a bright future.

That's when Mary and John made the smartest decision of all: they engaged a business broker to help them determine their exit strategy. They were only in their early 40s at the time, and their company's best days seemed ahead — why on earth, you may be wondering, would they be thinking of getting out?

The capacity to stay ahead of the curve is what differentiates successful business owners from wannabes, though. The partners realized that, with so much time still left on the retirement clock, this was the time to begin intentionally configuring the business to create maximum value. Over the course of several months, they mapped out their ideal retirement lifestyle and what it would take to achieve and maintain it. They even worked through tough issues like family succession.

They discussed the need to stay engaged in the business for a period of time post-sale, and what that would feel like. Finally, they talked about prospective buyers, specific dollar amounts and how best to position the business over the next few years to attract the best bids.

By thinking ahead, creating a plan and then working the plan, Mary and John built a foolproof leprechaun trap. A few years after they began planning their exit strategy, they were able to sell the business to a large multinational with very deep pockets. The key was "reverse planning," which we talk about elsewhere in this book — in their case, they picked their exit point (factoring in the requisite "earn out" stipulated in most agreements for purchase and sale) and their target value and worked back from there. What would it take to create that value in that timeframe? How did that subsequently impact both strategic business decisions and daily operations? Sales and marketing? Branding?

Mary and John were pretty astute operators, and I haven't seen many business owners live up to their example. But their story shows that it is possible to find that elusive pot of gold . . . provided that you take your time and build your leprechaun trap well in advance.

A QUICK PRIMER ON BUSINESS VALUATION

There are a number of ways to value a business. I prefer to use the projected annual cash flow from the business into the future, discounted by an appropriate rate to yield a Net Present Value for the business. Usually the projection should be carried forward for a reasonable period (five to 10 years, say) and then a residual value (assuming, of course, that nothing changes in the rate of growth of the business beyond the end point of your projections) added to the value determined for the period of your near-in projections.

Whoa! That's a mouthful, eh? It's about this point that I dive for cover and ask my finance guru to help out. Discounting cash flows and running financial models is not my forte, and it may not be yours either. That's OK — there are a number of good people out there who can help you, perhaps even someone in your firm. The important thing is simply to understand the rationale behind the model. With that in mind, let's walk through the basics:

Step One: Establish a Base Case. This is a forecast for the company's value at its current rate of growth. (Conversely, if the business is declining, you need to forecast a continued decline at the same rate.) The purpose here is to get an accurate assessment of the business. *No wishful thinking allowed!* Apply a ruler to five years of performance. Whatever it indicates in terms of a direction for growth, that's what you must reflect in your base business projections. It is what it is — there's no magic allowed for the "hockey stick" effect of sudden business improvements.

Step Two: Establish a Value for Synergy. For anyone contemplating buying a business, synergy cuts two ways. Positive synergy covers all the things that I could do as a purchaser to improve the value of the business by reducing cost as a result of the purchase. If I buy your company, for example, I can eliminate duplication across what will be our combined business and cut costs. It may be something as simple as reducing back office redundancy or selling excess land. Or perhaps my current manufacturing capability is more efficient than your company's, so supplanting yours will result in a cost reduction on the new combined P&L.

It could be that the combined volume of the two entities allows me to leverage more scale in purchasing.

Negative synergy must also be considered, however. I might need to build a new plant to house the combined volume or rent a larger space to house the additional people. There may be salary discrepancies between the two companies that must be resolved, costing me more in the short term. I likely will also have one-time costs associated with the purchase, some of which may be significant.

The goal of Step Two is to determine the cash flow impacts (short and longer term) of both the positive and negative synergies and to net them into one number per annum, which can then be discounted in the same way as the base case to provide a Synergy Value.

Step Three: Build a Value for Growth Initiatives. The final step in the valuation process is to determine a value for growth initiatives. Unlike synergies, growth initiatives are not proven, simply possible. From a seller's standpoint, these are ideas for growing the business beyond the constraints of the base case: unrealized potential of some undeveloped intellectual property, growth strategies currently unachievable because of capital restrictions, an untapped new market, etc. Any idea that has a reasonable chance of success could be considered a growth opportunity, really.

From a seller's perspective, the more tangible the idea, the more value it likely offers to a prospective buyer. From a purchaser's standpoint, the best growth opportunities are those avenues that they would not be able to pursue without the purchase. Each growth initiative can be presented as a potential add-on in terms of value (discounted cash flow again), the total sum of which is subsequently discounted by a risk factor (since not all these ideas will be realized).

PUTTING IT ALL TOGETHER

Based on that three step process, the valuation equation looks like this: *Base Case + Net Synergy + Growth Opportunity (discounted) = Total Business Value.*

Of course, in the real world you are unlikely to receive total value for your business in a sale. Your job as the seller is to create value, to try to persuade the prospective buyer to pay for as much of the synergy and growth opportunity as possible. To optimize your return, target *strategic buyers* — a buyer with a similar business system to yours or one that believes a unique growth opportunity will be created through the purchase.

The value of your business is higher to a strategic buyer than to others, since the purchase will allow them to combine the businesses for greater profitability and/or access growth opportunities previously unavailable to them. As a result, they are more likely to pay more to acquire your business.

Financial buyers are the "buy low, sell high" firms, usually the private equity companies who are regularly on the look out to buy, build (or reduce inefficiencies to improve cash flow) and sell. Their formula is generally to buy at lower profit multiples and then flip their investment within a defined time frame, usually no more than five to seven years. From a value standpoint, you're much better off focusing your efforts on attracting strategic buyers.

KEYS TO ACTION:

1. **Establish your "when" and "how much."** Use the "reverse planning" concept we talk about in a later chapter to identify your ideal exit strategy. When would you like to move on? How much will you need to sell the business for in order to support your lifestyle? Until you can quantify your goals, there's no way to determine if they are realistic — or what it will take to achieve them.

2. **Get a reality check.** Based on your desired purchase price and timeframe, determine how the business must perform over the intervening time in order to create the necessary value. Does that reflect the current performance of your company? If not, you've got some re-evaluating to do. Either you're going to have to change the way you're doing business, or you're going to have to adjust your expectations.

3. **Identify prospective purchasers now.** Can you build your business to make it more attractive to these specific candidates? Consider better aligning your business with theirs in order to create possible positive synergies or growth opportunities. You might even try to become a competitive irritant; for deep-pocketed companies in particular, it's sometimes easier simply to buy out a competitor than to deal with them year after year.

4. **Reverse role-play.** If you were one of those prospective purchasers, what would be an incentive to you to up the ante in any potential acquisition? Try to see the synergies and growth opportunities from their standpoint and run the numbers. Doing so will not only help you better develop the business' value, it will also help you negotiate a better deal.

5. **Ask for a second opinion.** Use a couple of trusted advisors to help you build a reliable estimated value for your business. Relying on a few expert opinions rather than relying on your own hunch will result in a more realistic appraisal of where you are and where you will be.

6. **Keep your eye on the leprechaun.** Keep tabs on prospective purchasers to ensure that your initial assumptions remain valid. Update your analysis and valuation model frequently to keep it current.

The Company Elephant

The ability to leverage "corporate memory" is increasingly vital for organizational growth, market differentiation and even economic survival.

Apparently elephants really do have terrific memories, just as the old wives' tales always said. A study on wild African elephants published a few years ago in the journal *Science* reported that the dominant female elephants that lead the herd build up social memory as they age.

"Elephants can certainly build up a memory over the years and hold on to it," study team leader Dr. Karen McComb told BBC News Online. "The matriarch plays a key role, because she has time to build up a social knowledge, and the others depend on her."

The matriarchs signal the rest of the herd whether an outsider is a friend or foe, allowing family members to focus on feeding and breeding when there is no danger. The older and more experienced the matriarch, the more adept she is at recognizing old friends, and the more calves the family is likely to produce.

If the matriarch, with the herd's most developed memory, is removed, the remaining animals are significantly more exposed to the threat of poachers and other dangerous situations. Memory was found to be critical to the herd's very survival.

CORPORATE MEMORY

Every organization, old or new, has a legacy. Properly leveraged, this legacy can be of tremendous help in creating market differentiation and brand awareness; it can, in fact, even become the foundation on which the company builds its future success.

Until fairly recently, companies could fairly easily access this collective memory in the form of knowledgeable, long-serving employees — you know, guys who collected a gold watch at their retirement because of their years of service. They were the corporate equivalent of the elephant matriarchs, possessing not only a vast store of information but also a kind of instinctual knowledge of the company's traditions, values and mythology.

But those venerable guardians of organizational legacy are members of a dying breed. Downsizing, retirement and death have steadily gutted their ranks, gradually robbing corporate America of its collective memory. As the baby boomers enter their golden years, we will soon see the greatest exodus of knowledge from the workplace that has ever occurred.

Companies who fail to create a viable plan for preserving their organizational knowledge in the face of these threats are courting disaster. As with elephants, the corporate herd's chances for survival are markedly reduced once the matriarch is removed.

Fortunately, there are some forward-looking companies taking steps to prevent that. One that I have had the pleasure of working with over the past few years has added several particularly strong programs to its mix. In addition to the standard "high potential" ratings ascribed to various individuals during succession planning exercises, the company leadership has also created two additional designations: "high professional" and "mentor." The "high professional" designation is for a person who demonstrates extraordinary knowledge within a particular area. While they may not be destined for a corner office, their role in the organization is nevertheless deemed to be critical. Examples include someone with an encyclopedic knowledge of key industry rules and regulations, or an engineer who has deep knowledge of the workings of a manufacturing facility. The designation allows the organization to recognize "strategic" talent and knowledge.

The "mentor" designation is unique, identifying those few individuals who represent a walking history of their department or even the entire company. They are the "go-to" people able to provide context or knowledge about company actions. In short, they are the company's mentors. I haven't seen another organization formally recognize and cultivate mentorship in quite this way, but based on the success the company has enjoyed, perhaps more should consider doing so.

This company also takes a novel approach towards its retirees by establishing a real community of retired employees. This community serves two needs. First, it permits the retirees to maintain ongoing virtual relationships with their peers. Second, it gives the company an active link to those "herd matriarchs," allowing them to be called upon if the need arises. I think that this is a particularly innovative — and inexpensive — way to ensure that corporate memory is not lost!

WHY DIDN'T ANYONE TELL ME?

I learned about the importance of corporate memory early in my career through an embarrassing but invaluable lesson. I had been tasked with preparing a budget request for research on a particular product that the company planned to introduce later that year. Eager to make a good impression, I immersed myself in the process, trying to gain insight into the current situation from a competitive and market standpoint. I spent hours preparing the request itself, writing and rewriting until it sang. With a flourish,

I handed it to my boss and waited for his praise to roll across his desk.

About midway through the research request, he cleared his throat and looked at me over the top of his glasses. "So, Bruce, tell me: have you gone to the research library and read the abstracts regarding the previous work done on this project?" he asked softly but pointedly.

Abstracts? What abstracts? Why hadn't anyone told me that there was prior research before now? I mumbled an excuse while my stomach flipped over sickeningly.

"Well," he said, "I'd like you to take the next couple of days, find that research, read it . . . and rework your proposal."

Not exactly the reaction I was expecting. I slunk out of his office, dejected, humiliated and angry. I was also determined as hell. I went back to my office and over the next few days found not only the research he mentioned but also a veritable treasure trove of information that had been filed away and forgotten for years. Thanks to what I found, I was able to rewrite the proposal in record time — and, truth be told, it was a much stronger one than what I had originally created.

Ironically, I did receive praise for my revised research request, constructed as it were on the shoulders of giants. But the lesson I learned, and the one that has stuck with me throughout my career was that we should always look back before looking forward.

The case for maintaining corporate memory isn't hard to make, just hard to implement. Every executive knows that his firm has built up a tremendous store of knowledge over the years, from "hard" technical information to "soft" organizational relationships and anecdotal experiences. Tapping it regularly can improve information sharing, reduce ramp-up time for new employees, lower cross-functional barriers, facilitate new learning and preserve lessons learned. But knowing the benefits isn't the same as knowing *how* to reap them. Listed below are some tips for putting your organization on a path to preserve (or even recapture) its heritage.

KEYS TO ACTION:

1. **Build a formal knowledge capture and retrieval system for both "hard" and "soft" data.** More than simply a raft of detailed reports, this system should be able to accurately "recall" what the reports contain. It should include file notes, correspondence, contracts, lists of people associated with programs, speeches, etc. Each report "area" should be prefaced by a summary of its contents for quick access.

2. **Focus.** You won't be able to record everything, so you need a master plan that determines what specific information your organization deems to be critical. This will likely include core information common to most businesses (financial data, research, etc.) as well as industry-specific information.

3. **Determine how you will use the information.** One way to help determine what information to capture is to think about how you will likely use what you collect. Who will be most likely to use the information? Where? For what purpose? This thought

exercise will help ensure that you retain key information while discarding the nonessential clutter.

4. **Determine a schedule and a common format for memory storage.** There will be a natural flow to the times that best serve your organization for capturing key information. Financial reviews, industry measurement (e.g. Nielsen), project completions, capital requests and the like generally follow a specific schedule. Build on that schedule rather than create something new. "Soft" data capture also has common break points, such as personnel movement, retirement and exit interviews.

5. **Identify the sources of the information, both "hard" and "soft."** "Hard" data is usually easier to collect, since facts and figures are easily recorded or filed. To collect "soft" knowledge, however, you'll need another collection methodology. The best way is usually a face-to-face session facilitated by a skilled interviewer using a mix of open- and close-ended questions. A recording device may be helpful for back-up and to avoid misinterpretation.

6. **Communicate and inform.** Your system won't be worth much if it isn't widely used by your employees. Both the importance of the process and the ability to access and contribute must be widely understood and widely supported. Use will create the value.

What's Your Type?

More than simply a corporate culture, your company has a unique personality. Understanding — and using — that insight is critical to a strong marketplace identity, alignment of purpose and sustained growth.

One of the most popular characters from the science fiction TV series *Star Trek: The Next Generation* was the android Data. Not only was he superhumanly strong and virtually indestructible — his positronic brain was capable of storing vast amounts of information and processing it in milliseconds.

In one of the series' early episodes, however, Data was ordered to submit to a dangerous Starfleet research project that would require him to be deactivated and disassembled. He refused and tendered his resignation, only to be informed that as an android, he was considered the "property" of Starfleet and had no right to resign his commission. He asked for and received a court martial to determine if he was indeed a sentient being.

The upshot of the trial is that Data was able to demonstrate that he fulfilled the essential requirements of sentience. In the eyes of the law, he is both machine and man.

BEYOND CORPORATE CULTURE

In the real world, the legal precedent for attributing certain rights to companies was set in 1886, when the U.S. Supreme Court ruled in the matter of *Southern Pacific Railroad v. Santa Clara County*. In a dispute over property taxes, the railroad claimed that the Fourteenth Amendment's "equal protection" provision prohibited the California county government from taxing it at a different rate than other companies. Southern

Pacific argued that since corporations had long been referred to as "artificial persons" — necessary in order to grant them some sort of legal status in order to pay taxes, to sue or be sued, and to own property — and the amendment did not specifically distinguish between "artificial persons" and "natural persons" (human beings), they too were entitled to its protection. Corporations might be artificial persons, said the railroad, but they were persons nevertheless. The Court agreed: companies are people, too.

A great deal has been written in the last few years about corporate culture. Very little, however, has been written about the personalities of these "artificial persons." But in my view they clearly have them. If I mention company names like Apple, Procter and Gamble, Johnson and Johnson, or Four Seasons, I'm guessing you'll immediately associate them with some signal trait or adjective: innovation, thoroughness, care, luxury.

Taking it a step further, I'd be willing to bet that if we both wrote a paragraph about our perceptions of the personalities of companies like IBM, Virgin, GE or Starbucks, we'd end up with a pretty similar set of descriptions. Now think about your company. Can you write a paragraph describing it as a person? What would happen if you asked a representative sample of your employees to do the same? What would they write? Would the core content be similar for each?

Believe it or not, the answers to these questions have far-reaching implications for your business. Being able to present "one face" to your employees, customers and suppliers is a sign that your company has a strong and fixed identity. Chances are that your in-market communication and execution are well integrated and your messages, both direct and indirect, are congruent and delivered consistently. In short, your company "personality" is rooted, and your stakeholders know what to expect from you and how to interact with you.

In my experience, a company's personality is indistinguishable from its corporate culture. As individuals, our values, behavior, and daily actions stem directly from our personality. The same is true for companies. Companies afflicted by an identity crisis are inconsistent, even schizophrenic. Their customers often abandon them when their expectations are unmet. They find it difficult to attract the right employees and harder still to retain them. Their growth is stagnant.

In a white paper entitled "Discovering and Living a Company's True Personality," Sandra Fekete makes the case for why corporate personalities matter: "Most people who encounter Disney's imagination, Nike's drive, IBM's methodical dependability or Nordstrom's service are in touch with what these organizations project every day. They know who they are – and they behave that way consistently. Successful, enduring companies have at their core a personality that we connect with and understand. In fact, all companies have a personality – because companies are people too. The trouble is, most companies don't know who they are. Once a company knows *who* it really is, the answers to questions like 'Where are we going?' and 'How do we get there?' become clearer and the path to success is more easily navigated."

A company that knows itself and stays true to that corporate personality derives a number of important practical benefits, Fekete argues, including:

- A strong sense of identity and alignment;
- A common language;
- Continuity and consistency in messages and behavior;
- Ability to deliver expectations consistently;
- Ability to identify and retain ideal customers and staff;
- A strong framework for decision-making.

HOW WELL DO YOU KNOW YOUR COMPANY?

Long after I had left my previous position at a Fortune 500 company, I happened to bump into one of our long-time marketing services suppliers. It didn't take us long to start talking about the "old days," and pretty soon I was reminiscing about my previous employer. Maybe a little nostalgically, I spoke glowingly about how proud I was that we, unlike most other companies that size, had always treated our suppliers well.

My former supplier looked me dead in the eye and snorted derisively. "On what planet were you?" he asked scornfully. "You guys were just as bad as the rest. In fact, several times your company asked us for a proposal, only to use the ideas we pitched while awarding the job to someone else. Other times we weren't paid for work performed. You guys weren't the worst, but you weren't any paragons of virtue, either."

I was stunned — especially because the group responsible had reported to me. The "personality" that I had worked hard to foster and had been so careful to model was caring, considerate and highly ethical. Obviously, though, there had been quite a difference between the collective personality I perceived and reality . . . and if not for an accidental encounter with my old supplier, I might never have known. As it was, I still didn't find out until it was far too late for me to effect any changes.

I like to think of myself as a hands-on and perceptive manager, so the fact that I was clueless about how my organization was actually behaving probably signifies a fairly widespread phenomenon. I'd guess that many, if not most, leaders are oblivious to at least some of the inner workings of their organizations. Who knows what damage was done and what opportunities were missed because of my group's bad behavior. I feel sick about it even now.

Direct customer contact is even more critical, as I myself experienced one recent Saturday. Walking into a certain high-end department store in all my weekend glory — jeans and t-shirt — I could immediately feel both the ritzy atmosphere and a strong aura of disapproval. I had the feeling that nobody was really welcome here, even those with the financial means to frequent it. It was as though the store was doing me a favor by allowing me to shop there.

A scan of the sales staff seemed to confirm that impression. To a person, they checked me out . . . and found me undeserving of their time and attention. I wandered the store un-served until finally one unlucky salesperson quite literally bumped into me.

"Can I help you?" he asked curtly. From the derision in his voice, it was clear that he thought someone dressed like me had no legitimate reason to be in the store.

"No thanks — just looking," I responded in kind. A few moments later, I left the store with no desire to ever return. I did have a strong desire to share my experience with my friends, all of whom easily fit into that store's desired customer wealth profile. The attitude of the sales staff, rather than helping select the right customer target, had actually alienated and damaged future business prospects. And I'm betting the manager was just as oblivious as I had been towards my old marketing supplier.

COMPANIES ARE PEOPLE, TOO

I think one of the reasons the concept of corporate personality hasn't generated more buzz is that, on the surface at least, the concept seems hazy. Soft. The linkage between a corporate personality and the bottom line at first glance seems tenuous at best. But this "soft" concept has some very hard edges.

Sandra Fekete, author of *Companies Are People Too*, has successfully adapted the Myers-Briggs Type Indicator as a matrix from which to determine corporate personality. The MBTI is a very well known and widely used tool for building a picture of an individual's personality type. It is based on a theory developed by psychologist C.G. Jung that most seemingly random variation in individuals' behavior is actually quite orderly and consistent. It results from basic differences in how people prefer to use their perception and judgment. In this context, perception refers to awareness about things, people, happenings or ideas; judgment involves how we reach conclusions about those perceptions.

According to the *MBTI Manual: A Guide to the Development and Use of the Myers-Briggs Type Indicator,* there are four dichotomies of basic personality preference:

1) *Favorite World.* Do you prefer to focus on the outer world (extroversion) or on your own inner world (introversion)?

2) *Information.* Do you focus on basic information and facts to draw conclusions (sensing), or do you prefer to interpret and add meaning (intuition)?

3) *Decisions.* Do you look first to logic (thinking) or at the people and special circumstances involved (feeling) when making decisions?

4) *Structure.* Do you prefer when things are decided (judging) or when they remain open to further options (perceiving)?

The permutations and combinations of each of these dichotomies yield 16 basic personality types. And as anyone who has taken the MBTI can tell you, it's a remarkably accurate tool for describing basic personalities.

What does that mean for a company? It's critical for ensuring that you hire individuals who will be good fits in the corporate culture. Beyond that direct application, however, understanding certain key predilections can help identify potential trouble areas. If your company is naturally introverted, for example, customer service may not come as easily to the organization as it does for a more extroverted company; you may need to devote more resources and training to ensure it doesn't slip.

A company that scores high in the "sensing" area may need more information to make a decision or formulate a plan than an organization that relies on "intuition." While that methodical approach has its advantages, it may also result in decision paralysis when clear facts aren't available (or in the face of information overload). The more intuitive company, though, may jump too quickly at perceived market opportunities or new technologies.

It's critical for your ultimate success or failure to understand why and how your company behaves the way it does. Your product or service may be the fundamental reason customers beat a path to your door, but how you deliver that product or service is an important differentiator. What personality is evidenced through your actions, processes and focus?

Isabel Myers-Briggs knew how valuable self-knowledge was for an individual. "Whatever the circumstance of your life," she wrote, "the understanding of type can make your perceptions clearer, your judgment sounder and your life closer to your heart's desires."

Think your business could benefit from that as well?

KEYS TO ACTION:

1. **Start with a test exercise.** The exercise is best conducted as part of a retreat or planning session. Ask each participant to write one paragraph describing the company as a person, then collect and share the responses. Talk about the perceived strengths and weaknesses, and discuss the implications for the company and its future actions. Ask yourself whether the output was consistent with your ingoing thoughts — did the exercises yield any surprises? Ask your team members to consider the impact of the exercise on individual plans and activities going forward.

2. **Employ a trained facilitator.** Because this area is so subjective, differences of opinion will most likely surface. A trained facilitator can help draw out and resolve differences of opinion productively. A third

party can also more easily get the group to step beyond the influence of office politics and boardroom speak and have some real, substantive discussion. Remember, only real talk yields real benefit.

3. **Broaden the exercise commensurate with perceived value, experience and confidence.** Make no mistake about it — this is risky stuff, even at the executive team level. Frank discussions outside the boardroom can breed expectations about the speed and scope of change that are unrealistic in the short term. To ensure that the exercise has a positive impact, you must educate the participants about its purpose.

4. **Consider using a personality profiling tool like Myers-Briggs for the individuals on your team.** This can be extremely valuable for both the individuals involved and the team as a collective unit, facilitating a deeper understanding and providing an objective base from which to talk about team and individual dynamics.

5. **Ask each team member to complete the profiling tool while role-playing the company as an individual.** Consider this is an alternate method for generating the same kind of dialogue as the first "Key to Action." It will yield many of the same benefits with the added advantage of a consistent "schematic" and language. It also offers linkage to the individual profiling segment.

Plan on a Page

When it comes to strategic planning, you don't need a plan the size of the Yellow Pages to be effective. Building a "Plan on a Page" could be the difference between business success and failure.

"Bruce," my boss told me with one of those cat-got-the-canary smirks that signalled trouble ahead for yours truly, "we've got a little challenge that I'd like you to take the lead on. As you know, we've just acquired a billion dollar company; I want you to oversee its integration — in addition to your normal day-to-day responsibilities leading your division, of course. I think that your experience in the mergers and acquisitions arena, as well as your previous role as head of strategy, makes you perfect for this assignment."

He stopped for a moment to let the information sink in, and I tried not to let my face show the initial stab of panic I was feeling. A billion dollar integration into a multi-billion dollar enterprise? What were they thinking? I had no integration experience. Weren't there consultants like Bain or McKinsey that did this kind of stuff for a living? Heck, what's a couple million in consulting charges when you're dealing in the billions? Were we suddenly going bargain basement?

After a decent interval, I responded. "Sure," I replied, hoping my voice sounded more confident than I felt. "Sounds like an interesting challenge."

What I didn't tell him was that I had no earthly idea how I was going to succeed in such a daunting task. But as it turns out, necessity really is the mother of invention, and that trial by fire proved the impetus for the creation of an incredibly simple, pragmatic and powerful tool: the "Plan on a Page."

Since that experience, I have used the Plan on a Page process to successfully help companies ranging from start-ups to billion dollar enterprises; I even use it for personal goals. I have discovered that it yields clarity, continuity of focus and alignment on objectives among even strikingly diverse groups. The people and companies who have used it now tell me that they swear by it — some have even called it a godsend!

The Plan on a Page is the cleanest way possible to get to great in-market execution and performance. It's built with simplicity and effectiveness in mind, particularly in order to help avoid the kind of pitfalls I'd experienced in more complex corporate planning processes. And thanks to the "test driving" that it's received over time, it has been refined to an even more streamlined, focused and effective level.

In just a moment, we'll get to the "how's" of creating your Plan on a Page, but first . . .

WHY PLAN?

This number never ceases to shock me: over 85 percent of small and medium sized businesses work without a formal, written plan. Why do so many of us resist business planning? The reasons are as varied as the businesses themselves. Consider these examples of the most common excuses I hear:

- "Too much effort."
- "Planning takes time away that I could be spending on my core business."
- "The plans just end up gathering dust on a shelf, anyway."

- "We already know what we have to do. There's no point in wasting time writing it down."
- "We're too small to need a plan."
- "I just haven't gotten around to it."
- "I've never found these business plans remotely useful."
- "I don't know how to do it."
- "We already have one: our budget."

On the other hand, it's been shown repeatedly that businesses with a formal plan, although not guaranteed of success, nevertheless on average outperform their peers that lack a written plan. Planning results in a number of tangible benefits, including:

- Stronger and more robust top line growth.
- Enhanced bottom line performance.
- Improved alignment and common focus.
- Commonly understood key objectives and deliverables.
- Improved resource allocation.
- More clearly defined operating and project priorities.
- Identification of high-level key challenges.
- Establishment of an "early warning system."

The case for planning is very clear-cut. Less so, for most companies, is the type of plan that should be created. I worked for a long time in an organization that seemingly specialized in formulating the most comprehensive strategic plans on the face of the planet. In their detail and their complexity they were practically works of art!

They also engaged a significant number of people from across all the areas of the company for extended periods of time. Planning formats begat other formats in a complicated schedule of development and review, starting at the lowest level in the organization and working up to the top over a period of literally months. Plan templates had to be revised for *each* level of review, including endless revisions and re-writes. The total number of company man-hours spent in this endeavor was absolutely mind-boggling!

Finally, the plan was presented to the highest level in the organization, approved and parked in everyone's credenza. Ah, the plan was complete! Just in time to start the process over again . . . Sound familiar?

On the other hand, I just left a client who owns an advertising agency. We happened to be speaking about his business and got around to the subject of planning. "Do you have a plan?" I asked. His head dropped and his eyes avoided mine.

"No," he replied. "And I'm embarrassed to say that in virtually 100 percent of our contact with our clients, we advise them to build a plan. Few have them when we first work with them. I guess it's like the cobbler whose children go without shoes."

Sadly, that is a very common theme — 85 percent common, I'd guess. And that's why the Plan on a Page works. It's simple, and it gets used.

THE TRUTH ABOUT STRATEGIC PLANNING

If you've worked for a large organization for any length of time, I'm sure you've run into a similar version of the "Endless Plan Syndrome." It was precisely this experience that sparked my intense distaste for a protracted planning process and which finally prompted me to seek another avenue for the planning process. What I discovered is that underlying any planning are some simple but profound truths:

Much, if not all, of the answer is already known to the organization. How many times have you heard the lament that the majority of consultants just mine for information that already exists within the company and parrot it back? To some degree that's true. The collective knowledge of any team is a powerful thing, and the sheer number of years of industry and business experience represented by a planning group is usually impressive. It's also almost always more focused than any outside resource. In my experience, the key to good planning is not an exercise in new thought, it's the discovery and unlocking of information already held. The answer, my friends, is not blowing in the wind — it's been with you all along.

Communication and sharing are arguably the major benefits of a planning exercise. Put another way, it's as much about the journey as it is the destination. Regardless of the size of firm we work in, the ability to come together and problem-solve is critical to quality of a plan and its execution. The process allows each team player to represent his or her area of expertise while simultaneously gaining a holistic view of each other's contributions to the entire company.

The process is best facilitated by a third party. Whether an "insider" or someone contracted from outside the firm, the facilitator must be regarded as impartial, having no vested interest in the outcome of the exercise and no agenda to favor one particular group over another. An experienced third party facilitator can also more easily and tactfully ask certain "politically incorrect" questions while also smoothing over any rough edges that emerge between people and functions. He or she can also challenge the participants to ensure that group-think doesn't take hold of the process. (The last person who should ever drive the process is the CEO or owner!)

Participants must understand the exercise's purpose, process, timing and individual expectations. As Stephen Covey said, "Start with the end in mind." In order to fully engage the participants, they need full information about why this process has been developed and how it will affect them individually and collectively. Knowing that information ahead of time will help them commit to the program. Without this important step, the planning process — not to mention the input and output — will likely be flawed. If possible, it is beneficial to engage an outside-in perspective (such as a key customer, supplier or shareholder) to help ensure that the planning input is balanced.

Knowing the proposed process ahead of time is also critical, since the participants must be able to build this new activity into their ongoing work. Setting the expectations and establishing the process in advance yields improved commitment to the process. This step should also include the opportunity for participants to provide input and ask questions in advance, which will usually result in increased commitment.

The time set aside for the planning process must be focused and short. Most people see planning as tangential to their primary job: to execute. The greatest risk associated with planning exercises is that the process becomes unwieldy and excessively bureaucratic, eventually suffocating under its own weight. The best planning process is quick, requires minimal pre-work from the team and results in very clear actions, timelines and accountability.

Each project identified must have a single owner. There can be no joint accountability. Each project must have one name — and only one name — associated with it so the team understands whose responsibility it is to deliver.

The plan must be measured. That which gets measured, gets done. The team must also understand and buy in to what is being measured; if they feel that the measurement is beyond their influence, or if they don't know how they each contribute, the process loses efficacy. Bottom line: they must see themselves and their impact on the plan.

So let's begin . . .

BUILDING YOUR PLAN ON A PAGE

You can build your Plan on a Page in just seven simple steps:

1. **Identify your planning team.** *Share both your "end in mind" and the process itself.* This is a critical step. For the sole proprietor, it's pretty easy — just look in the mirror. For all others, the key is to ensure that you engage all the people who are likely

to own the execution of the plan, as well as anyone likely to have significant knowledge for input.

The double-edged danger here is either engaging too many people or too few. Too many and the process can bog down; too few and the process can be criticized as "elitist" as input becomes too restricted. It is also important to consider a 360-degree process, which optimally engages both inside-out and outside-in perspectives. Most planning processes, from what I've seen, are deficient in addressing the latter. You can solicit that critical outside-in perspective in a number of ways: an "insider" with access to an outside-in perspective or a more formal outside-in review (customer feedback, for example).

Once you have identified your planning team, hold a separate meeting in order to share the goals for the exercise, the full process and the responsibilities of the team. Because this exercise will be seen as incremental work, you must also take the opportunity to outline its benefits and help the team understand its importance. It may even be beneficial to remove or reallocate some of their day-to-day responsibilities.

2. Develop a shared view of where you stand today. This step develops a "SWOT," helping you identify your Strengths, Weaknesses, Opportunities and Threats in order to develop a shared view of the company's present condition. Strengths and Weaknesses form the "internal view," while Opportunities and Threats outline the company's external environment.

Individual pre-work comes first. Ask each participant to separately complete a SWOT exercise. Doing so helps guard against group-think in the first planning meeting and encourages candid, unbiased thinking. Once the individual assessments are complete, the group should meet to develop a collective SWOT. The individual assessments should be reviewed and used to create a master list (this can be done in advance of the group meeting or as part of it).

This first group meeting (always facilitated by a third party) is an engaging process whose end product is a holistic and united view of the company's current position. Formulate a two or three sentence SWOT summary to represent an "elevator-speech" version of your situation. In the exercises I run with my clients, I refer to this as the "FROM" statement. You are going to move FROM here to somewhere else: your destination.

3. Develop a shared view of where you're headed. Once you have a complete picture of where you are today, you can commence the process of identifying where you want to go. This is the stage in which you will paint a picture of what the company (or you) will look like at the end of the planning timeframe.

The objective of this step should be to write a one-sentence description of that eventual goal: your destination. Although this sounds easy, it is in fact the toughest part of the exercise and involves a lot of dialogue. It must be something that each employee — or each external stakeholder, for that matter — can understand and embrace.

Combined with the SWOT summary (the "FROM" statement) this picture of your future is the "TO" portion of a "FROM – TO" statement. Together they form a simple thought that synthesizes the company's strategic intent and direction.

4. Identify your gaps/success factors. Once the team has developed an understanding of where the company is and where it should be going, they need to take a hard look at what's needed to get there, developing a list of the things that must be done or overcome. The company may not be able to address all the needs immediately (usually because of resource constraints), but it is still very beneficial to identify the key obstructions or needs; doing so keeps the company from being blindsided later by either an unrecognized need or the sheer scope of the undertaking. It also helps frame the work plan and aids in the identification of those areas requiring further work. This activity helps recognize the mountain that is to be climbed for the organization and also brings into focus the key steps required to deliver the plan.

5. Build the plan's key thrusts (strategies) and the projects or actions that support them. This sounds more daunting than it actually is. The first step is to identify the key areas and broad strategies that will form the basis for the work. In my experience, there is usually a common group of broad themes:

- *People:* There is usually a "people goal" associated with propelling the organization toward the end goal.
- *Growth:* Which projects/processes are key to driving the top line?
- *Customer:* Who are they? Profitability? Focus?
- *Production:* Building products or services that deliver value.
- *Processes/Practices:* Core processes that create effectiveness and efficiency.

Once specific goals for these or other broad areas are discussed and agreed upon, the team should develop a "to-do list" of specific projects required to accomplish each goal. Assign no more than three to five activities per key thrust.

6. Assign one owner to each activity. See the previous section for the necessity of avoiding joint accountability.

7. Identify the Key Performance Indicators (KPIs), tracking mechanisms and review timing. This step allows you to outline those core measurements you will be using to track your progress toward the end goal. Examples may include revenue growth (percentage and absolute), cost reduction targets, cash flow, customer profitability or churn, employee satisfaction; margin growth, share, share price, etc.

Congratulations — your Plan on a Page is now complete! Properly formatted, you should be able to include the key output from this activity on one page. A sample of a one-page plan, the workbook and starter questions are provided in the appendix of this book for your review and use.

PUTTING THE PLAN TO USE

Building the plan is just the start, of course. While it's useful in getting people thinking about the present, the future and the actions required to get there, the real benefit of the Plan on a Page process is its power to align and help focus activity on a daily basis. Believe it or not, your plan should be reviewed daily, whether you've built it for yourself as a sole proprietor or on behalf of a billion dollar corporate behemoth.

The plan should become the source of your areas of focus, dissected according to annual, quarterly, monthly, weekly and even daily activity. It should be a living, breathing document that helps everyone decide what work needs to get done — and even more importantly, what doesn't. It should outline who is doing what for whom and for what reason; if it isn't on the list, it shouldn't be done. If it needs to be put on the list, you should hold a discussion to decide either what should be deleted or delayed to support the addition, or what other resources should be committed to accomplish the project. Use your Plan on a Page as a benchmarking tool in your key status meetings. Are you progressing? How is each of the projects coming along? Are you on track to meet your objectives and KPIs?

This process works so well because it is so simple and clear. Even better, it is not restricted to size or purpose. It serves as a personal "life plan" just as effectively as it does to plan the activity of a Fortune 500 company — I know because my clients and I have used it for both.

Enjoy your new tool, and happy planning!

PART THREE

Leadership Fog Lights

"You are the organization you must master."
– Stuart Heller, Author

Life in the Rear-View Mirror

The clearest paths are set from your destination to where you stand today.

It was no secret; our team had simply not performed up to the company's expectations. Despite the presence of some very talented individuals, we had struggled to find a shared identity and deliver consistent results. Even our few successes had been marred by backbiting and back room gossip.

So when team leader Bob stepped forward at a meeting, we all expected to be royally chewed out. Instead, he suggested an exercise he told us would help not only diagnose the problems that faced us, but also discover solutions.

"Take out a piece of paper," Bob instructed us. "On the top line, write today's date — a year from now. Got it? Now, I'd like each of you to write an 'obituary' for this team. Include the cause of 'death,' the key events leading up to its demise and some of the efforts to sustain the team along the way. On the flip side, include some highlights of the team's 'life.' What were its accomplishments? Its disappointments? How will it be remembered. You have five minutes; then we'll discuss the results."

That was my first exposure to "epitaph planning," a powerful tool for taking control of your destiny by imagining the end goal first and planning backward to the present.

NEW YEAR'S RESOLUTIONS

If you're anything like me, you're more willing to talk about planning than actually put pen to paper. In fact, years of expert procrastination in this area eventually resulted in a seven-step program I've perfected for my New Year's resolutions. I'll bet you've got a similar process:

1. Resolve that this New Year is going to be "different."
2. Create a mental list of your top three goals for the coming year, ideally focusing on health/weight issues, family time and business success.
3. Commit your goals to memory rather than write them down. (This is key.)
4. Allow yourself to slip back into the daily grind.
5. Break first resolution by mid-January; feel guilty for two or three days afterward.
6. Let weeks and months pass.
7. Repeat process next December 31st.

Truth be told, I was always a little suspicious of people who actually wrote down their personal goals and held themselves accountable to them — seemed a little new-age or Tony Robbins-esque to me, I suppose. So Bob's little team exercise brought a grimace to my lips . . . at first.

I have to admit, though, as I sat there and listened to what the other team members had written, it made me reevaluate. It made me rethink how we communicated our ideas, how we approached projects, how we treated each other in and out of the office. I suddenly saw the potential we were squandering because of petty personal differences and shortsighted decisions. I saw all the "coulda-beens" and "shoulda-beens" laid out without adornment or apology.

It was a disturbing but effective experience. I realized then and there (and I wasn't the only one) that the only way to fix the problems in the team was to radically shift our perspective. Imagining the epitaphs that people would assign to us accomplished what no tongue-lashing or group rah-rah session ever could — it made me (and our team) genuinely commit to making some needed changes. Like Ebenezer Scrooge imploring the Ghost of Christmas Future for a second chance to alter his miserable fate, our team drew a deep collective breath and hoped there was enough time for us to create a different, and profoundly better, epitaph for ourselves.

In the years since then, I've tried to more consciously analyze activities both personal and business from that same end-first perspective. What will the epitaph be? Am I (or we, in the case of a team) satisfied with it? What steps need to be taken to get to the goal-line? As business guru Stephen Covey once advised, "Start with the end in mind."

THE REVERSE PLAN

A one-time colleague of mine definitely lived by his version of the "reverse plan." Henry was a typical Aussie: bluff, good-natured and quick with a joke. He loved the good life and made the most of every opportunity to carve himself a big piece of it. And he was a sports fanatic. So his "reverse plan" started with him listing on a sheet of paper the top ten sporting events (World Series, Super Bowl, the Masters, etc.) that he planned to have seen in person before he retired, which gave him about a ten year window.

He conservatively planned to cross off at least one event per year. But with his goals concretely established, he ended up meeting them well before his window closed. "Wait," the skeptics among you are saying, "planning to go to the Super Bowl isn't the same as setting a goal of financial independence or aspiring to the top position in a company or developing a successful new product! All he needed was a credit card and a calendar!"

I'll grant you that Henry had a pretty simple goal — but he also gave himself a pretty rigid timeline. And as a VP of Human Resources, making the time to travel to these events wasn't as easy as you might think. The point isn't Henry's specific goals, though; it's his approach. He mentally projected himself ten years in the future and asked himself: "What will I have accomplished in the last decade that's important to me?"

Reverse planning means starting at the end, defining what you want to have accomplished and working yourself back to the present. At first, adopting this kind of outlook can feel a little awkward. Most of us have trouble with planning, anyway. Life gets in the way. Business or personal, we're in survival mode much of the time. Our "plan" becomes myopic in scope: landing *this* client or increasing sales *this* quarter and simply making it through *this* week.

But the ability to define your long-range goals, personal and professional, and then work backward to identify the individual milestones necessary to achieve them is an invaluable technique. In fact, it's often the difference between actually achieving those goals and ending up with a life or career filled with regrets and missed opportunities.

MEANS TO AN END

A friend of mine who happens to be a financial planner excels at helping her clients see their lives through that lens. Unlike most of her peers, she avoids talking about specific financial goals with prospective clients. "Most people aren't interested in a financial plan because of the numbers," she told me. "They're just interested in the things they can do with the numbers once they're there. Money is just a means to an end — better house, independence, comfortable standard of living — not the end itself."

Kelly steers the talk away from numbers during initial meetings, focusing instead on life goals. Surprisingly, those are hard for a lot of folks to articulate. She estimates that only about two percent of the people she interviews have established specific long-term life goals. Two people out of every hundred! The remaining 98 had only a vague notion of what they wanted out of life. I can tell you that the numbers for smaller businesses aren't that much different! Personal or professional, we could all stand to step back and plan in reverse.

By helping those clients first clearly identify their goals, Kelly found that the financial planning itself became simply a matter of working backward to determine what financial steps had to be taken and when in order to meet those ultimately non-financial goals.

So where do you fall? Are you one of the two percent . . . or the 98? What do you really want out of your life? Your business? When it's time to reminisce to your grandkids, what stories do you want to be able to tell them about what you've done, where you've traveled, who you've met?

To be blunt: what will your *legacy* be?

KEYS TO ACTION:

The process described here is also covered in the chapter entitled "Plan on a Page." In this instance, think about your life plan.

1. **Identify where you are right now.** Start with a SWOT (Strengths, Weaknesses, Opportunities and Threats) assessment of your current situation. Strengths and Weaknesses focus on the internal factors (you and your family situation); Opportunities and Threats deal with external factors. In what areas do you excel? Where is there room for improvement? What advantages do you see in your current situation?

2. **Identify your destination.** The SWOT analysis establishes your starting point; this step summarizes your eventual goal. Think of this as your "epitaph statement." It should encapsulate what you want to accomplish.

3. **List three to five areas of focus.** What shorter-term activities will lead to the achievement of the long-term goal you identified in step two? Where will you need to concentrate your efforts? This is a life plan, remember, so don't limit yourself to purely financial or professional goals. Consider some of the following areas:

Artistic	Rest and Relaxation
Relationship	Public Service
Charitable	Education
Physical	Financial
Family	Travel

4. **In each area, list activities to be completed.** Identify up to three projects or activities that contribute to the achievement of the areas of focus. Basically, this is a fancy "to-do" list driven from the end goal. Identify the key areas you will track to ensure you're making progress — what gets inspected gets respected (and completed).

5. Congratulations! You've just completed your first personal plan. **Now place it next to your bathroom mirror** so it's the first thing you see every morning. As you shower, shave, brush your teeth or get dressed, read it again. In addition to the zillion other things that are already going through your mind for the day ahead, think about the one or two things you need to do to stay committed to your personal plan. Make yourself accountable — and enjoy the results!

Fire in Your Belly

Passion is the prerequisite for success, in business and in life. Neglect yours at your peril.

Journalist Carmine Gallo has interviewed some of the leading lights of business, men and women who have changed the landscape of business — and made themselves a pile of cash in the process. And yet, he says, money is rarely their primary motivation. Few successful businesspeople speak of a passion to get rich. They do, however, eagerly speak about their passion for their company, product, service or customer base.

"I've interviewed several entrepreneurs who have joined the billionaires club," Gallo says. "I've watched them address staff, customers and investors. Not once did they ever discuss how much joy they get out of being wealthy. Instead, they talk about the passion they have for their business . . . through stories, anecdotes and examples."

Gallo cites an interview with Starbucks' founder Howard Schultz in which the coffee entrepreneur talked about his mindset. "You must have a tremendous love for what you do, and *passion* for it," Schultz told him. "Whether I'm talking to a barista, a customer or investor, I really communicate how I feel about our company, our mission and our values. I've said this for 20 years – it's our collective passion that provides a competitive advantage in the marketplace, because we love what we do, and we're inspired to do it better."

GOALS VS. VISION

Not long ago I was working with a client to help him shape his company's future. The business was already successful, but this exercise was designed to help solidify his goals and create a plan for bringing them to fruition. What, I asked him, was his vision for his business.

(Let me stop here for a brief editorial aside. I absolutely *hate* the word "vision." I've spent way too much time with groups that labor endlessly over what does and does not constitute a vision, and as a result I've been "visioned" to death. Instead, I prefer the word "destination." That's an image that's easier to get your head around and, in my experience, doesn't cause a group to de-evolve into esoteric discussions. Despite that, I'll continue using the word vision because most are familiar with it.)

"My vision for this business is to do $400 million in revenue by 2015," he said solemnly.

"That's a terrific goal," I told him. "But it's not really a vision. Let's try looking at it another way: I'd like you to think about your passion and try to put that into words."

"OK," he said, pausing for just a beat or two. "I'm passionate about building this company to $400 million by 2015."

"Let's try this one again," I said. "Why did you start this business in the first place?"

"Well," he said, "back when I was in college, I was working as a painter and saw that the guy who owned the company consistently did pretty lousy work. I thought that our customers were getting a pretty poor bang for their buck. A lot of times, they were elderly and he was really taking advantage of them.

"Watching him, I decided that I wanted to start a painting company, staffed by university students, that would be dedicated to providing the highest quality at a reasonable price. The people who hired us would not only get a good product, they would know that they were helping young people through school. I wanted it to be a win-win situation for both our customers and students."

"Aha!" I interrupted him. "So you were passionate about providing great service to your customers while helping your student employees fund their education. Right?"

"Yeah," he said. "I see where you're going now — my vision had nothing to do with the money. The money was a by-product of the vision and my passion for it."

Entrepreneurial guru Guy Kawasaki has taken companies to task for writing formulaic, boring, business-speak vision statements. Instead, he says, a good vision statement should be like a mantra for the company: short, emotionally-charged and capturing the essence of what the company was trying to accomplish. It should be a living reminder of what the company stands for and what it aspires toward, something that will inspire, energize and challenge.

How many mission/vision statements have you read that live up to that ideal? Yeah, I thought so. But I think Guy's point is valid. Truly great companies are differentiated by the enthusiasm and devotion of its employees. That was certainly true at Apple when he worked there developing the first Macintosh computers; programmers cheerfully worked hundred-hour weeks because they were caught up in something larger than themselves. They believed their product would revolutionize the personal computer industry — even society itself — and they desperately wanted to be a part of the crusade.

Do your employees look beyond their paychecks? Do you? Is there a collective sense that the work you're doing is worthwhile, necessary, beneficial? Do you have a shared passion for a common vision?

MIDLIFE CRISIS

Tom was a pretty normal guy from a pretty normal family. He grew up in a middle class community, graduated from high school with slightly above average grades and enrolled in an arts program at a public university.

He changed majors a couple of times, but his focus was directed more towards parties and co-eds than academics. Sure, every time he was home for the holidays he had to field questions about what he was going to do after graduation, but he never let it worry him. There was plenty of time, he reasoned, for him to figure out what he wanted to do with his life.

Midway through his final semester, he awoke one night with a panic attack. Heart racing, he suddenly realized that he was coming to the end of an era. The "real world" was just around the corner, and he had no clearer idea what he wanted to do than he'd had three and a half years before. Spurred on by that gnawing feeling of anxiety, Tom began to take things a little more seriously and was grateful when, after graduation, he was offered a job at a large, reputable company. They paid him a decent wage and for the most part he liked his co-workers. Tom relaxed, and the panic attacks stopped.

The days stretched into weeks, the weeks into months and the months into years. Tom married and had a couple of kids, bought a nice house in a nice neighborhood, moved into middle management. Life seemed pretty good.

And then the panic attacks started again.

This time, Tom realized that his anxiety wasn't financial — it was emotional. Despite its superficial comfort, his life was unfulfilling at some more basic level. Tom tried to dismiss it, but the anxiety refused to go away. Finally, he came to terms with his feelings: more than anything, he wanted to quit his corporate job and open his own store.

Still Tom hesitated. Sure, maybe that was his passion, but he wasn't a young guy anymore. He had a family to provide for, a mortgage to pay, a certain comfort level to which he'd become accustomed. Could he really risk all that?

Then a co-worker, a man just a couple of years older than Tom himself, died suddenly from a heart attack. After the funeral, Tom took stock of his life in a new way. What if he died? What would his legacy be? What if he was on his deathbed looking back over his accomplishments? Would he be filled with pride? Contentment? Regret?

Tom took the plunge, quit his job and opened up a store. Now, several years later, he owns a small chain of retail outlets. He is reinvigorated, passionate and happy — wealthy in the truest sense of the word. Every day is an adventure.

I'll bet that most of us know someone like Tom . . . with one critical difference. Our "Tom" never went on to start that store. Instead, he (or she) stuck with the familiar, hoping just to endure until retirement. God forbid, that "Tom" might even be us.

Passion is the common foundation on which success, real success, is built. It can't be ignored, faked or disguised. You can see it in the eyes of the entrepreneur pitching a new idea to prospective investors, in a doctor describing a revolutionary new procedure, in a teacher eager for the first day of a new school year. It's real — and it's powerful.

PASSION STARTS WITH YOUR HEART, NOT YOUR HEAD

"Great," you may be thinking. "But there's just one problem — I don't know what I'm passionate about!"

Relax. According to an online survey conducted recently by none other than Oprah Winfrey, over 70 percent of us have no idea where our passion lies. My 18-year-old daughter summed it up the other day when she asked me, "Dad, what should I do? I don't know what I want to be." Hell, I had no idea what I wanted to be when I was her age, either. I was interested in a whole range of things, but I can't honestly say that I was passionate about any of them.

The first step in finding your passion is recognizing that you can't intellectualize or force your way into it. Think about a great love in your life — the butterflies in your stomach when you saw them, the way your heart pounded when your hand brushed theirs for the very first time. Now think about another relationship that seemed ideal on paper — similar interests, great conversations, common values — but never seemed to generate the same spark of passion. No matter what your mind says, the heart wants what it wants . . . in romance and in life.

I was recently recruited for a leadership position for a major charity. Thinking about how my experience and skill set might benefit the organization, I sat down with the recruiter for a long interview, confident that I was the right guy for the job. But during the interview, I began to feel somewhat detached.

Listening to myself talk, I realized that although I was saying all the right things, I wasn't speaking with the passion of a believer. I hadn't been touched personally, in any way, by the particular disease that the charity had been founded to combat. I was speaking with my head, not my heart. I quickly withdrew my name from consideration.

Discovering your passion can take time, patience and courage. But take it from me, the benefits far outweigh the risks. Wouldn't you like to wake up each morning excited about what the day will bring, eager for its challenges and opportunities? I know I would!

KEYS TO ACTION:

1. **Create a "passion inventory."** What do you enjoy doing? Make a list, including even the things that seem unrelated to business. If money weren't an issue, how would you spend your days? What interests and goals would you pursue?

2. **Create a "skill inventory."** Visualize a mental highlight reel of your best moments and most significant achievements. What are the common denominators? What skills allowed you to reach those successes? List them, ranking them in the order of their importance to those achievements.

3. **Poll others.** Sometimes others see things more clearly than we do ourselves. Enlist the help of those close to you — friends, family, mentors, co-workers — and

ask them what they've observed about your passions and skills.

4. **Test market.** Sometimes you just have to experience something to make an educated judgment about it. Consciously step outside the comfort zone of your normal activities and try some different things on for size. Just remember to check your ego at the door.

5. **Ask yourself the most fundamental question of all: "What makes me happy?"** Deep down, you probably know already what your heart wants. The hard part is sometimes coming to terms with it, especially when it involves risk or change (or a reduction in income). But until you can honestly align your life with the answer to this question, that "fire in the belly" feeling will likely elude you.

The Machine Stops
Build "high touch" into your "high tech" communication efforts and increase your effectiveness.

I first read E. M. Forster's "The Machine Stops" nearly 35 years ago, and I think I've grown to appreciate it even more in the intervening years. Written in 1909, it's a prescient story about a future society in which most humans live in individual "living compartments" buried far below the planet's now inhospitable surface. Each person is provided with all they need to live by a vast machine, which also connects them to others.

Over the years, the humans begin to revere "The Machine" and the cocooned, artificial existence that it has provided for them. "Unmechanical" malcontents are threatened with expulsion to the feared surface; the few humans who choose to live there are seen as uncivilized barbarians, little better than animals.

Despite the advantages of the underground society, the central character, Kuno, chafes at its artificiality. He confides to his mother, Vashti, that he has snuck out and visited the surface and seen the humans living there. Vashti is horrified, unable to imagine an existence unconnected to The Machine and the rest of her cocooned brethren.

But Kuno warns her that one day, "The Machine will stop." Almost against her will, she begins to see defects and breakdowns in its operations, growing slowly but inexorably more serious and widespread. Humans long ago lost the knowledge required to repair The Machine, so they can only watch helplessly as more and more functions fall silent. Eventually, The Machine fails completely. In the society-killing chaos that follows, Kuno makes his way to Vashti's shattered cell — the first time mother and son have physically touched since his birth.

As they wait to die, they realize that mankind's connection to the natural world has been at last restored. The Machine's artificial constraints destroyed, it becomes clear that it is the surface dwellers who will rediscover the old ways and rebuild the human race.

BLACKBERRIES IN THE BOARDROOM

"The Machine Stops" predates television, videoconferencing and the Internet by decades, but it sure captures the paradox that accompanies major innovations in communication technology: the more we advance, the harder it becomes to hang onto the "human factor" when communicating with each other.

Communication is faster and more pervasive than at any other time in mankind's history. Once it moved no faster than the speed of sound (our voices); often it moved only at speed of the fastest horse or the swiftest-sailing ship. But here, on the far side of the new millennium, it moves literally at the speed of light. Once only a handful of people in any given town possessed phones; most of you reading this likely possess a handful of phones: home, business, cordless, cellular.

I've done business with people in Japan and not thought twice about the ease with which we had discussions, shared documents and collaborated on common issues. A generation ago, it would have taken a week's worth of telegrams to accomplish what email lets me do in an hour. Around the world in 80 days? I can send an email or make a phone call to virtually anywhere in the world in less than 80 milliseconds.

What's the downside, you ask? A business acquaintance of mine deals capably with that very issue in her consulting practice. She speaks of how the blending of phone and Internet technologies in the past two decades have inadvertently created a whole new set of communication problems. The fact is, we're biologically hardwired for face-to-face communication, relying a lot more on visual cues like facial expression and body language than on the actual content of what's being said. Stripped of the benefit of those cues, we're a lot more apt to misunderstand others, inadvertently give offense or lose focus. "We message more and communicate less," as she's fond of saying.

What's really dangerous is the strain that "media mixing" can put on our professional relationships. I've seen that firsthand with that most insidious of machines: the BlackBerry. It's a great concept, but so easy to misuse.

Just the other day, I was speaking (face-to-face, dinosaur that I am) with someone when his BlackBerry chimed at the same moment I bent down to pick something up. Oblivious, I continued speaking — but when I straightened up, I saw that he had retrieved his BlackBerry from its holster faster than any Wild West desperado and was already thumb-typing. "Huh?" he grunted, still riveted to the tiny screen. "What were you just saying?"

Another time, I was sitting in the boardroom of a Fortune 500 company to hear several hours of presentations. Many of the presenters were clearly nervous, but it was apparent they had really slaved over their displays. At one point, I happened to glance around the room and was horrified by what I saw.

Probably half the executives there were busily answering emails. A couple of them were smiling from ear to ear, presumably at some joke emailed to some of the group from one of the other executives present. The poor presenter knew she'd lost their attention, but what was she to do but gamely push on and pretend she was unaware of what was happening. I could almost see her wilt, and it made me furious. Access to "faceless" communication media had made my fellow executives profoundly disrespectful of actual face-to-face communication. (Eventually, by the way, we were able to institute a "no BlackBerries in the boardroom" policy. It was not, as you may guess, universally applauded.)

I used to own a BlackBerry. But I finally gave it away — it was simply too tempting to answer that alluring little buzz, no matter where I was. I felt like I *had* to know who was emailing me *right now!* It might be important, damn it! I was becoming addicted (that's why users jokingly refer to them as CrackBerries) and it was damaging my focus during face-to-face contact.

So if you must have a BlackBerry, exercise restraint in how and where you use it. Don't sacrifice *communicating* for the sake of *messaging*.

MAKING RIPPLES

Businesspeople aren't unaware of the problems that result from such prolific but impersonal communications tools. They know the value of a firm handshake and a face-to-face exchange, and through the use of new networking groups they've tried to address the challenge of making real, human connections in this digital age.

The networking groups have soared in popularity over the last few years, particularly among business owners and service providers (usually SMEs). Typically, they're held in a hotel or restaurant setting and designed to allow folks to talk a little shop and swap business cards with others, hopefully laying the foundation for future business opportunities.

But for a lot of businesspeople, these events feel a little hollow. That's what prompted Steve Harper, author of *The Ripple Effect*, to rethink the methodology of networking. He saw few real connections — and, as a result, few legitimate opportunities — created in a typical networking event. The communication was simply happening at too superficial a level to begin the process of building real relationships.

So Steve developed an event that he has termed the "Eight Minute Ripple." Key to his approach is that everyone has to discard their business "mask." Participants are discouraged from sharing their business title or description; instead, interactions start on a personal basis with descriptions of your personal life, hobbies, family and dreams. The intent is to help participants to get to know each other as people first, and businesspeople a distant second. Put another way, it's designed to facilitate connecting with people, not personas.

Steve's model is a wonderful example of the good things that can happen when we re-establish the human factor in our communications. Participants report having more genuine interactions and, true to Steve's theory, ultimately creating more mutually-beneficial opportunities . . . as well as friendships. It's a little unnerving to ditch the professional masks we habitually wear in public, but it seems to be the key to forging authentic relationships.

The bottom line is that technology can be a wonderful tool, but a terrible master. I love email and cell phones and unlimited long distance as much as anyone, but I have to remind myself that they are only a means to an end. The fact remains that at the other end is a human being, not a machine. There's a person beyond the persona. Reaching that is the goal of real communication.

KEYS TO ACTION:

1. **To humanize your communications, first re-establish mastery over your communication devices.** Whether it's your BlackBerry, cell phone or other like device, you must resolve to selectively banish the offending items. Take it off your belt during those times when you really don't need it (more than you think). Put it in your briefcase when you get home and during those times when you're interacting with others, like lunch or while you're at your kids' hockey game. Make it a business hours-only connector.

2. **Walk, don't type.** It's a lot easier to type a note to someone these days than to get out of your chair and stroll down the hall to ask a question. It used to be that "management by walking around" was a good thing. It still is. Do it whenever possible.

3. **Take a writing course.** Most of us (including me) assume that we are good communicators. I have discovered, however, that I'm not as good as I think

I am; what appears to me to be clear communication isn't necessarily the case. Renewing or strengthening our skill base by getting a little extra help via coaching is a good thing.

4. **Close the communication loop.** This must happen from two perspectives: yours *and* theirs. Cycle back to ensure that outbound communication is understood by those receiving it, especially when the message is an important one. Don't just assume that you have been understood. The same goes when receiving a communication; mentally play back a summary of what you think is being communicated, and clarify anything that is unclear or confusing. Doing so will help keep you from assuming something that is not the case, which in turn may help avoid potentially costly errors.

5. **Avoid business speak.** Why do most of us begin speaking what sounds almost like another language once we hit the business environment? Is it because we think it makes us sound smarter? Because we feel we need buzzwords to fit in? Avoid the jargon as much as possible; pretend you're talking to your best friend, your mother or a neighbor. Simple language is the cleanest, best way to convey your thoughts.

6. **Learn the appropriate channel etiquette.** There are a myriad of "do's and don'ts" for each means of

communication (all caps in email is perceived as "shouting," for instance). Learn them to increase your communications effectiveness and avoid faux pas. If you're over 30 and feeling a little out of your depth, ask a teenager. Seriously. They grew up with this new technology and often understand the appropriate etiquette better than we do.

The Shackleton Way
Group hugs can kill. In the end, leaders must lead.

The British Trans-Arctic Expedition (1914-1916) is one of history's most famous "successful failures." Led by veteran explorer Sir Ernest Shackleton, the expedition's goal was to cross Antarctica on foot — 1,800 grueling miles across one of the most inhospitable landscapes on the planet, a frozen desert blasted by gale-force winds and temperatures colder in places than the surface of Mars. But less than a day's sail from the continent, the expedition's ship became trapped by massive ice floes. Soon the *Endurance* was frozen tight in the impenetrable ice, where it remained for 10 months!

Unable to free the *Endurance*, Shackleton and his men watched helplessly as the ice eventually ground it to pieces. They were marooned on sheets of floating Antarctic ice over 1,000 miles from the nearest civilization with only three lifeboats and some supplies scavenged from the doomed ship.

The men had different notions of the best course of action. Some wanted to strike out in one direction, others in another; some were ready to simply give up. But Shackleton refused to allow the expedition to become paralyzed by dissent. He laid out a course of action and promised his men that if they all followed his lead, they would survive.

Under Shackleton's guidance, the men dragged the lifeboats across the shifting ice floes for another six months. Eventually the ice became so unstable that the expedition was forced to take to the boats, finally landing at Elephant Island, a dismal little rock covered by penguin guano and lashed by storms. Knowing that his men were nearing the end of their rope, Shackleton then took the best boat and a small group of followers and set out for a whaling station on South Georgia Island.

When they landed, having survived an 800-mile journey across arguably the worst seas on earth (and nearly swamped by a hurricane), Shackleton discovered they were on the opposite side of the island from the whalers. Currents made it impossible to try again, so Shackleton resolved to take two men and cross the mountainous interior of the island — despite having no climbing gear.

Against seemingly insurmountable odds, Shackleton and his men did reach the whaling station, and with their help returned to rescue the men trapped on Elephant Island. Amazingly, all of Shackleton's men survived in reasonably good shape.

Years later, when a researcher asked First Officer Lionel Greenstreet how the men survived such an ordeal, he answered in one word: "Shackleton."

SELF-FULFILLING PROPHECY

"If you're a leader, a fellow that other fellows look to," Sir Ernest Shackleton once said, "you've got to keep going." That simple philosophy flies in the face of so much of the current take on leadership best practices, though, which tend to emphasize concepts like "social" leadership, "emotional IQ" and "consensus-building" and empowerment."

Many leaders assume that if employees are unhappy, it's their responsibility to make them happy. Sounds harmless enough, eh? The problem is that that approach is usually based on a false assumption that the grumbling you hear represents a majority view. But I'm here to tell you that it usually doesn't — quite the opposite, in fact. In my experience, most companies are saddled with a small but vocal group of constantly discontented employees. You know the type: people who seem happiest when they're complaining about something.

Usually, by the way, they're also your least productive employees. Shackleton noted that the most pessimistic members of his expedition not only contributed less than the others, but also ended up in worse physical shape. He definitely saw a direct correlation between positive outlook and eventual result, and he knew pretty early on which men he could count on and which were little more than baggage.

If you don't identify these grumblers for what they are, it's easy to spend an inordinate amount of time, money and corporate energy trying to placate what you perceive to be the unhappy majority. As a result, you wind up neglecting your true business focus in a short-sighted attempt to build "employee-centered" or "win-win" programs.

Worse, pouring all this attention onto the perceived negative situation actually creates a self-fulfilling prophecy. "Wow," say employees, customers and vendors previously uninfected by the grumblers, "they wouldn't be spending this much time and money on this unless it really was this bad." Before long, the negative minority really has become the majority. Welcome to the spiral effect.

CONSENSUS GONE WILD

About 10 years ago, one company with whom I was associated embarked on an effort to effect some significant organizational change. It started out as a very well-intentioned program and ended up as a cautionary tale about why consensus building on a broad scale is so often such a lousy idea.

The company, once a leading light in its industry, was mired in flat profits and zero growth. Several of their key customers had become competitors, usurping the company's power position within the value chain and torpedoing their status in the industry. Within a very short time, it appeared that the fundamental rules of the game had changed.

To find a solution, the CEO decided to embark on a strategic planning exercise: assess the situation, identifying key strengths, weaknesses, opportunities and threats; then shape a vision, mission and a set of strategies that would guide the company to the promised land. Nice idea, right? The problem was that he decided to include the whole company in this exercise. The whole company. Over 2,000 employees!

His expectation was that every group within the organization, from the executive suite on down, would produce their own "functional" strategic plan. Since he held firm to the belief that company leaders should work on, not in, the business, he mandated the executive team spend — no kidding — at least three weeks every month working on the new plan. Yeah, they sure weren't working in the business anymore; they'd basically abandoned the business in favor of an artificial world of jargon, acronyms and insular concepts. They became irrevocably distanced from the rest of the company.

When they finally emerged from the holy smoke of planning and thinking, they held lengthy, days-long sessions with a "leadership team" comprising the top 100 employees, who were asked to analyze, critique and offer revisions to the executive plan. Then they went through the same process with each of the company's functional groups (marketing, sales, finance etc.). They even engaged outside stakeholders!

What had looked so good on paper became a real-life nightmare. The incessant drive for consensus consumed the company. Meetings lasted late into the night. Almost no meaningful work — the kind that might have actually helped rectify the situation — was being done. And employee morale plummeted. The win-win scenario had become a lose-lose reality.

The CEO who had spawned this brainchild was finally unceremoniously shown the door, leaving his successor to try to clean up an even bigger mess. And the lesson I learned? Sometimes, consensus kills.

"LEADERS LEAD"

That's the bottom line. It doesn't mean that consensus isn't a good thing to have (it is) or that morale-building activities aren't sometimes nice (they are). But in the final analysis, it's your responsibility as a leader to shape a vision and lead the company across the ice floes to solid land. It's your job to determine direction, establish goals and set expectations. You don't have to be nasty, but you do need to be the one out in front. "Don't be afraid to take a big step when one is indicated," advised the British statesman David Lloyd George. "You can't cross a chasm in two steps."

We all need a little reminder about leadership from time to time. I remember very distinctly a time I was admonished to get off my butt and lead. I was grappling with a particularly knotty business issue that involved significant risk to both the company and to my own career — if things went well, I'd be a hero, but if we missed the mark I'd be run out of town on a rail.

Paralyzed by indecision, I opted for a second opinion. I went to a colleague in another part of the company and asked her advice. She paused for a few moments. "I can't tell you what to do, Bruce," she finally said. "I can tell you, however, that "leaders lead."" Rightly chastened, I returned to my office and made the decision. To this day, I hear her words whenever I face a difficult challenge.

Leadership is not without risk. Shackleton and his men all survived their ordeal, but his contemporary Robert Falcon Scott perished in his quest to be the first to reach the South Pole. The history of exploration, in fact, is littered with the bodies of those who made bad choices — and the history of business is littered with the husks of companies whose leaders made bad choices. But that same corporate landscape also pays tribute to the visionaries who had the courage and conviction to venture where consensus would never have taken them.

"We must become the change we want to see," said Mahatma Gandhi. That "becoming" is a risky proposition for most of us. But without it — without real leadership — nothing worthwhile is ever achieved . . . in life or business.

KEYS TO ACTION:

1. **Start with "active listening."** All great leaders have the ability to listen intensely. They scan their environment and accept input from a variety of sources, particularly their employees and other

stakeholders. They suspend their own agenda and thoughts and build knowledge.

2. **Build consensus by asking for input.** Those who help build also support. That doesn't necessarily mean that you must take all input received, though. Even the simple act of asking — and truly considering — input will garner support even if the final decision doesn't line up completely with some of the input provided.

3. **Align yourself with productive employees.** They're usually the majority and will support you against the grumblings of a negative but vocal minority.

4. **Don't back yourself into a corner.** Nobody is right every time, all the time. Be bold enough to change your tune if you have been wrong . . . and be honest enough to admit it publicly.

5. **Be clear.** Once a decision is made, everyone in the company, from the corner office to the mailroom, must have the same understanding of the direction you're setting.

6. **Punt the naysayers.** Give people a chance to get on board. Get rid of those who don't.

Be an Archipelago

Gone are the days of holding your cards close to your chest. Future success will require we "open source" both our ideas and ourselves.

Robert was an exemplary employee. Conscientious, hard working and focused, he delivered on his commitments. He got along well with both his co-workers and those who worked for him, and seemed to have all the tools for moving up the corporate ladder surely and steadily.

But Robert had a hang-up. Almost ruthlessly independent, he hated, absolutely *hated*, asking his superiors or co-workers for help or advice. He was worried that he would be seen as a "suck-up." So he kept quiet.

What he didn't realize was that his pride had a price. Promotions didn't come as fast as he expected or, frankly, as fast as he deserved. Despite his skills, he didn't regularly register on senior management's radar, which meant he was often passed over for special projects and other opportunities to showcase his talents. The company didn't benefit from his talent and skills as fully as it could have, and Robert — as well as those around him — became increasingly frustrated.

As Robert's manager, I saw all this firsthand. I tried to convince him that seeking advice from those willing and able to pass along the fruits of their own experience wasn't sucking-up. I urged him not to try to go it alone. But my pleas fell on deaf ears. For Robert, receiving help was an admission of weakness, a fatal crack in his professional armor.

NO ONE IS AN ISLAND

"No man is an island, entire of itself," wrote the poet John Donne. Too often, though, that's exactly what we aspire to be: independent, solitary and aloof. We don't want to admit that we *can't* do it all, that we need a helping hand or an encouraging word of advice — and we're often reluctant to share our ideas, afraid that others will take credit for our creativity.

I know because when I started out, I felt a lot like Robert. I wanted to be seen as the young world-beater, not some wet-behind-the-ears rookie. Only with some hard knocks and real world scars did I gradually come to appreciate the importance of the input from others, especially mentors, and become willing to share the fruits of my experience. Best lesson I ever learned.

Many islands seem solitary. But beneath the surface, they are in fact geologically connected to other nearby islands. In the same way, our success is built on an archipelago of relationships with others in both business and life. Far from being a threat to our career, the open sharing of ideas, advice and experience helps cement the bonds of those relationships and almost always result in greater success than we would have achieved on our own. The old saw that "we're stronger together than we are alone" is a truism precisely because it's . . . well, true. And, what's interesting is that it is the culture surrounding the new technology of the Internet that is accelerating the social change.

The new reality requires that you take a risk and "open-source" yourself to co-workers, mentors, associates and others in order to succeed. Try to go it alone and you'll end up isolated or ignored.

STRIKING OPEN-SOURCE GOLD

Rob McEwen was the CEO of small and struggling Toronto-based gold mining firm called Goldcorp, Inc. With the company close to shutting its doors for good, Rob released $10 million to his geologists in a last ditch effort to discover tangible evidence of gold-producing land. Soon the scientists returned with tantalizing news: test drilling yielded a possible strike worth as much as 30 times the amount Goldcorp was currently mining! If they were correct, the find would save the company from financial disaster. Unfortunately, however, the results weren't conclusive enough by themselves to justify additional investment for a company so strapped for cash.

Inspired by computer programmer Linus Torvalds, (who released the source code to his revolutionary open-source Linux programming language to the world so that others could improve on or add to the original), CEO McEwen hit on an unusual — and seemingly risky — idea. He decided to make locating successful mining sites on the land into a contest for any geologist who cared to try his or her hand at it, offering $575,000 in prize money. To facilitate their efforts, he made public all the information Goldcorp had collected about the 55,000-acre property.

In the traditionally proprietary and secretive world of gold mining, this was an unprecedented step. Traditional industry experts pooh-poohed the idea, predicting disaster for the company. But McEwen was adamant — and desperate.

Turns out that he was also correct. Contestants from around the world and from many different disciplines turned their focus on the problem. The response and the quality of the input was far beyond expectation. (It was a new way of doing business!) Of the 110 target sites submitted by the contestants (many of which Goldcorp's own geologists had not identified), over 80 percent eventually yielded gold. Thanks to McEwen's bold open-source strategy, the underperforming $100 million enterprise grew into a $9 billion juggernaut.

BARING YOUR SOUL CREATES BUSINESS

Rob McEwen's story has a surprising postscript. Mary, the owner of a reasonably successful publishing house, decided to apply McEwen's example in a completely different context. Hoping to accelerate not just the growth of her business but also her own personal development, she emailed a summary of the major challenges she was facing in her professional and personal life to her entire address book. She asked the recipients to do two things: first, consider whether they personally could help or advise her in any of the areas she mentioned and, if so, to reply to her email; second, to forward her request to their own list of trusted contacts.

Mary nervously waited for the results of her email appeal. Would she be ignored? Ridiculed? She was all to conscious of the fact that she'd just bared her soul to the world. "Oh my God," she thought, "what have I done?"

She needn't have worried. Within half an hour, she'd received 20 replies and several referrals. By the following week, hundreds of people — some of whom she'd never even met — had emailed her with thoughtful advice and offers of assistance. Many of those contacts blossomed into long-term, mutually beneficial relationships, and her business prospered as a result. Her open-source risk had succeeded beyond her wildest expectations.

Even more unexpected, several of her correspondents began asking for *her* advice about *their* business challenges! Her unique approach, far from resulting in embarrassment, had actually garnered her the respect of her peers. They valued her perspective and admired her moxie; she became a thought-leader in the virtual community she had helped create.

MENTORS MATTER

Mary had done more than simply create a new type of networking. She had used modern technology to help rejuvenate an "old school" concept: mentoring. She had, in effect, created an entire network of virtual mentors.

There are a few fundamental, incontrovertible facts I've learned. One is that you won't succeed in business — or in life — without the help of mentors. The right mentor can help you avoid potentially devastating pitfalls, forge promising new connections, challenge yourself in areas you never would have explored alone, open your eyes to hidden lessons and deeper truths, and guide you along the sometimes tangled path to success. A good mentor is a jewel without price.

Mentoring isn't a one-and-done experience, by the way. It's a mindset to be cultivated. If it's true that we never stop learning, then it's equally true that we never stop needing mentors. In this information-age, technology-driven economy, isn't it more important than ever to have guidance accompany knowledge?

A good mentoring relationship really is symbiotic. Both people win. The student benefits from the mentor's experience, network of contacts and knowledge. But the mentor, aside from helping someone achieve their potential, also gains knowledge. Optimally, both parties are at some point in the relationship both mentor *and* student. Roles change over time, making the mentoring situation a relationship in the truest sense of the word. Mutual goals and values must be shared.

It's interesting, isn't it, that the Internet, the growth of virtual communities and the increasing popularity of open source philosophy are really helping reinforce some very traditional notions of the value of relationships. Whether you're an early adopter or a technophobe, though, do yourself an important favor: find and engage mentors. You won't regret it.

ROBERT'S REALIZATION

Remember Robert, whom we met at the beginning of the chapter? A few years ago I happened to run into him at a social function. After exchanging a few pleasantries, he suddenly became serious.

"I want to apologize to you, Bruce."

"Why?" I asked, genuinely taken aback. "We haven't even seen each other for years."

"Do you remember your advice to me about the need to reach out to others? How it wasn't sucking-up or giving other people a chance to steal your good ideas? How the relationship benefited both parties?"

"Sure," I replied a little cautiously.

"You know, I really disagreed with you at the time. Truth be told, I thought you were just being 'political.'" He paused. "I want to tell you that I was dead wrong about you and your advice. It took me a long time to really hear what you were saying. But I just wanted you to know that I get it now. Without your words echoing in my memory, I don't think I would have. Thanks."

For Robert's sake, I'm just sorry he didn't understand that sooner.

KEYS TO ACTION:

1. **Research mentoring, both formally and informally.** Use the Internet to research various types of mentoring available and establish some criteria for a good mentoring situation for you. Most governments, academic institutions and even some companies offer free mentoring services — discover what they have available and determine if it might be right for your needs. Also talk to your immediate contacts, especially those with large networks. Ask significant others, parents, friends and teachers about their mentoring experiences.

2. **Create a personal inventory of key goals.** What would you like to achieve through a mentoring situation? Identify key knowledge gaps you want to address or areas you'd like to strengthen.

3. **Create a mentor network.** The ideal situation is a network of mentors, each of whom offers a different set of skills and knowledge. Leverage your existing network to create some warm contacts with potential mentors in the appropriate areas.

4. **Don't label the relationship(s).** Like any relationship, a mentoring relationship has to develop naturally over time in order to really blossom. You can't force it. If it's working, you'll both know what it is without having to formally label it.

5. **Use the Internet as non-traditional relationship resource.** Again, focus first on your trusted contacts, friends and associates. Ask them how they use the Internet to address both personal and business challenges. Which resources have been the most helpful? Do they belong to any "virtual communities"? If so, what are they and how are they using them? Learn about blogs and other tools for sharing ideas, receiving feedback and connecting with others.

6. **Test a couple of approaches to "open sourcing" your ideas.** Remember, each individual's experience is likely to be different depending on their personal preference and their technical confidence. Go slowly and build on what works for you; drop or modify whatever doesn't.

7. **Make it a two-way relationship.** You've got to give to get. Providing feedback and input to your network of mentors will build the value of the interaction for both parties. Take the time to provide this feedback as part of the mentoring process and you will be rewarded.

Sweaty Palms

Differentiate or die! Success depends on standing out from the crowd. Playing it safe can actually be the most dangerous path of all.

While meeting with advertising mega-agency Young and Rubicam about a new campaign for Kool-Aid several years ago, I listened as a well-manicured young account rep laid out the agency's recommendation for the coming summer marketing plan. They planned a six-week series of summer TV commercials targeted at moms, promoting both the drink's appeal to kids and its affordability. It was the message we'd traditionally sent, delivered through a tried and proven medium.

I hated it.

"This is a very safe approach," I said during the expectant pause that followed his presentation. "But safe doesn't get you noticed. Risk gets you noticed. If our palms aren't sweating at least a little at the thought of what we're about to do, then we're not really doing our job."

The advertising folks looked at me, some shocked, some puzzled, some grinning slightly — thinking, no doubt that I was just giving back to them some of their own medicine. You see, it's usually the agency that cajoles the client into taking a higher risk, not the reverse.

"Let me give you an example of the kind of risk we should be taking," I told them. "Toblerone Chocolate is also one of our brands, and to market it our usual first thought would be to employ the same kind of TV campaign you're suggesting for Kool-Aid. But what if, instead of playing it safe, we spent that money dressing up Toronto's CN Tower to look like a giant

Toblerone bar! It would certainly stand a better chance of getting noticed – and not just in Canada, either, but around the world. If we're going to spend the money, let's at least make sure someone notices."

To their credit, the Y&R team took the challenge to heart. They suggested that we post the iconic Kool-Aid face in a number of colors (signifying the different flavors) in some very unusual places: on the sides of buildings, at the bottom of swimming pools, at crowded water parks, painted on sailboats in the harbor, even on train cars that crisscrossed the country.

Did they have sweaty palms when the presented this new idea? I'm pretty sure they did. But the success of the campaign exceeded even our most optimistic expectations; business boomed and worldwide advertising awards came flooding it. We took the path less traveled — the riskier path — and won big.

So why do companies so often do just the opposite?

PURPLE COWS AND BEIGE BOARDROOMS

In business, even in industries that pride themselves on innovation, there is a constant temptation to play it safe, to go with what's worked before, to tell higher ups what they want to hear. Don't. That's playing not to lose instead of playing to win, and it's often the difference between business success and failure. The fact is that every business decision carries risk, and sometimes it's the choices that seem safest at the time that, in hindsight, are the riskiest.

Peer pressure is constantly telling us to conform, to fit it, to go with the crowd. But wallflowers don't get noticed, and businesses that don't get noticed don't get customers. Chocolate towers or

Kool-Aid faces on trains, well, *those* definitely attract attention. Author Seth Godin captures that concept brilliantly in his book, *Purple Cow*.

"When my family and I were driving through France a few years ago, we were enchanted by the hundreds of storybook cows grazing on picturesque pastures right next to the highway," Godin writes in the introduction. "For dozens of kilometers, we all gazed out the window, marveling about how beautiful everything was.

"Then, within twenty minutes, we started ignoring the cows. The new cows were just like the old cows, and what was once amazing was now common. Worse than common. It was boring.

"Cows, after you've seen them a while, are boring. They may be perfect cows, attractive cows, cows with great personalities, cows lit by beautiful light, but they're still boring.

"A *purple cow*, though. Now that would be interesting."
Godin hammers home the point that success depends on being *noticed*. Sure, it feels risky. It can be uncomfortable. It may not even work the way you intend. But although getting noticed doesn't guarantee success, staying unnoticed almost always guarantees failure.

Purple cows don't always play well in the boardroom, though. Dollar-conscious executives, worried about squandering the company's money and their own job security, tend to water down the really bold ideas — ultimately, they're more comfortable with beige than purple. Beige is safe; it doesn't have sharp edges. And even if it doesn't help much, it certainly can't hurt.

You see the results of this kind of "boardroom advertising" all over the place. In fact, I'd venture to say that at least 75 percent of the advertising that's out there right now is boardroom advertising: boring, bland, banal and completely, utterly ineffective.

RISK IS YOUR BUSINESS

The same tension that exists in advertising between playing it safe and taking risks exists in other facets of your business as well, whether you're a billion-dollar multinational or a home-based start-up. Conventional wisdom is going to scream at you to stick to tried and proven ideas and methodologies; success demands that you get sweaty palms.

In an article for *Business 2.0* magazine, authors Michael V. Copeland, Paul Kaihia and Paul Sloan created a list of ideas for some international ventures that would definitely rank high on the sweaty palms scale:

- Building cheap Wi-Fi networks for Brazilian resorts.
- Becoming a bio-diesel producer in Argentina.
- Creating an ad network for India's mobile content developers.
- Launching an exclusive social network for Russian millionaires.
- Exporting the planet's next great wines – from Greece.

Out there? Maybe. But remember that every successful business was once nothing more than a gleam in their founder's eye. We now take Southwest Airlines' service model for granted, but it was a novel — and risky — concept when Herb Kelleher rolled it out. Dell's made-to-order computer delivery system was scoffed at by many self-styled know-it-alls, but it transformed the industry. IBM took a dramatic risk in reinventing itself from a purveyor of "hard" information systems to a consulting powerhouse.

Of course, only a handful of these kinds of transformative ideas ever see the light of day. Many, many more end up on the cutting room (or the board room) floor, as I've seen firsthand.

While working for General Foods early in my career, I was given an assignment in the company's lucrative coffee arena, where its dominant brands made it an industry powerhouse: Maxwell House, Sanka, Mellow Roast, General Foods International Coffee, Brim and Maxim were just some of the powerhouse brands. My job was to identify some exciting new ideas in the coffee market that could provide the company with additional paths for growth.

During my search, I stumbled across a new coffee business model in Europe: a company named Tchibo, founded in 1949 by two German businessmen. Tchibo served its coffee by the cup in small retail locations, but also sold it in packages for take-out. These small shops became informal community meeting places; people made it part of their daily routine to drop by and have a cup or two while reading the paper or conversing with friends.

"Eureka!" I naively thought. "This is a can't-miss idea." I promptly developed a business plan around the notion and sent it up the chain of command.

Given that General Foods never came to be known as "Starbucks," you can probably imagine what happened. "Too risky," my bosses told me tersely. "We are *not* in the retail coffee business."

It was a very understandable reaction to a fairly wild idea from a junior employee. The real question is how many of these ideas you are letting slide because you see them as too risky. But risk can be managed: start small but think bigger; test; play Johnny Appleseed with a number of ideas and see what grows. You don't have to bet the farm if you're smart about it.

I'll leave you with this post-script: at the time of this writing, Starbucks has grown to over 6400 locations worldwide. (Oh, wouldn't it have been nice?) If you want to stay in business, remember that risk is your business.

KEYS TO ACTION:

1. **Start by challenging the status quo.** Do the same thing and you'll get the same result . . . or worse. I once had a terrific boss who, when reviewing plans for the upcoming year, would ask as a standard question, "What's changed? What's new?" He understood that to improve results and grow the business, we had to do some new things. To get different results, you've got to try different things.

2. **Look to other successful business models as "thought-starters."** I'm a big believer that great ideas are usually repurposed thoughts reconstructed in new and unique ways. The "Toblerone Tower" idea came from my observation that some other companies were much better than we were at creating "events" that attracted attention. In today's Internet-enhanced world, it's much easier to search the global idea

reservoir for great ideas; even a little quality time on Google can set your mental wheels turning.

3. **Be creative, but stay focused.** Despite the need for some risk-taking, don't be different just for the sake of being different. New ideas must be tied inexorably and naturally to your business; they have to make sense to your existing or future customers. Case in point: the Kool-Aid idea, which tied the visual to kids having fun in the summer. The media was different, but it was still expertly aligned to the brand's essence: kids and fun.

4. **Keep the creative "input" down to a dull roar.** Ever get advice on decorating? If so, you know that you get as many opinions as the number of people you ask. Good, different ideas are just that — different. Spread your creative net too wide and you'll likely end up with a something that looks very conventional.

5. **Test it.** By testing it, you can take the opportunity to learn and modify the campaign, offering or methodology. Doing so helps alleviate unnecessary risk.

6. **Seek innovation in all your business processes, not just service or product offerings.** Some of the best ideas have nothing to do with your current offerings,

but can profoundly affect the way you do business. Expand your view of innovation to include your business processes.

7. **Don't stop.** If it ain't broke, fix it. Then fix it some more. There's always a way to improve on what you've got. Once you've got a win under your belt, go back to challenging the status quo and start over. Better still, make the process continuous — as in "continuous improvement."

Credit Paradox

Be a "credit mirror." The more you reflect and share the moment, the greater the return.

There's a great scene in the Christmas classic, *Miracle on 34th Street*, where a manager at Macy's department store overhears the new Santa Claus send a customer to Macy's competitor, Gimball's, for a pair of roller skates. The powers that be are understandably upset, and Santa is given the boot.

Then something unexpected — and wonderful — happens. Customer after customer shows up gushing about how wonderful this "new program" is, and how it shows that Macy's really cares about its customers. Once-a-year shoppers promise to become regular customers and pledge to tell all their friends about the "store with a heart."

Santa's quickly rehired, and what began as his personal crusade to de-commercialize Christmas spreads to department stores across the country, each ready to direct shoppers to other stores to find what they're looking for . . . all in the hope, of course, that in doing so they'll actually be winning hordes of loyal new customers themselves.

"PRAISE LOUDLY, BLAME SOFTLY"

The Russian empress Catherine the Great once advised: "Praise loudly, blame softly. Always give your people the credit for your achievements and success. Never take the credit for yourself, but take all of the blame."

What a counterintuitive concept in our hyper-competitive, get-ahead-at-any-cost world! Give away credit? How on earth am I going to get noticed, praised, promoted? And since I'm on the hook for the blame if things go wrong, why shouldn't I get credit when they go right? I earned it!

Perfectly natural feelings. Now ignore them. I know it's a paradox, but the reality is that by reflecting credit onto others, your standing with them will actually increase — as will your position within the company. Conversely, the more praise you unashamedly accept, the weaker your influence base will be.

Here's a real-life example. John was a tremendous contractor who built a very successful business over the years. But early in his career, he bought into the notion that the best way to build the business was to tout his accomplishments. He spent a lot of money placing ads in various media, citing all his happy customers and examples of his work as "proof" of his quality to prospective clients. His business grew, and he believed that his formula was a major reason why.

One of John's strengths was regularly reviewing and measuring the effectiveness of his various business development strategies. While reviewing customer information one day, he had an epiphany: the majority of his new clients had come through referrals, not advertising. His large advertising budget had been for the most part a waste of the business's resources.

But it made sense. Choosing a contractor can be an intimidating experience; nearly everyone knows someone who has an absolute horror story to tell about hiring the wrong guy. So what reassured prospects most wasn't slick ads, it was people who had themselves taken the same risk and come away satisfied. Their testimony carried real weight because they weren't profiting from the referral — if anything, they were risking their own reputation in recommending him. The most effective business-building tool, John discovered, is a qualified reference.

The principles that underlie that lesson apply equally well to dealings within a company. It's much more persuasive when people independently hear about the quality of your leadership, creativity or commitment than if you try to promote that image directly. And to facilitate that endorsement process, you have to consistently reflect the credit for accomplishments onto those around you. Trust me, they'll notice and they'll love you for it.

HOW TO SHARE CREDIT

Even when you've bought into the idea of really sharing credit, many organizations still struggle with the issue of *how* to compensate and recognize employees. Here's a tale of how two different approaches produced very different results.

Mary and Peg ran different departments within a large communications firm. As they entered the new year, they both struggled with how to appropriately reward their employees. Although being part of a monolithic company had certain advantages, in this case it was a minus. The HR department had decreed only a two percent average wage hike over the employee base. Not exactly something to get excited about.

Mary took more traditional approach, splitting her department into three categories: "High Performers," "Meets Expectations" and "Needs Improvement." She then budgeted compensation so that the "High Performers" received three or four percent raises . . . which were, of course, funded by the underperformers. On paper, it was a nicely balanced system. But she soon noticed that it wasn't having the effect that she had intended. Even the "High Performers" weren't all that enamored with their raise, while those who received even lower increases were upset without really being motivated to improve.

Peg, on the other hand, took one look at the situation and immediately foresaw the situation Mary found herself in. So she found a more innovative solution. Instead of taking the budget as-is, Peg sliced 10 percent off the top *before* she applied the compensation math. With that money, she started an "accomplishment fund." Throughout the year, she used it to purchase relatively inexpensive items — theater tickets, event passes, hotel vouchers, books, trophies, etc. — to reward outstanding performance. She called these her "pats on the back" and delivered them individually, along with a personal note of thanks, rather than center the rewards around some big group annual event.

And you know what? Peg's approach worked. Her employees appreciated the frequent personal gestures (which, incidentally, reflected very well on Peg's own standing in the company) and worked considerably harder for the "pats on the back" than they ever did for purely monetary compensation. This innovative means of recognizing others and sharing credit created a more productive, happier environment — and helped Peg move up the corporate ladder.

To paraphrase something U.S. President Harry S. Truman once said, "It's amazing what you can accomplish if you share who gets the credit."

KEYS TO ACTION:

1. **Be appropriately visible in recognizing employees.** The qualifier, *appropriately*, is important. It goes without saying that recognition should genuine and public to have any kind of positive effect; it should also be scaled in proportion to the achievement. Employees can smell fluff a mile away.

2. **Personalize the recognition.** Nothing says we care more than spending the time to personalize a message. It could be engraving the person's name on a plaque or something even simpler like a handwritten card or a phone call. If there's a way to link in co-workers and family, so much the better.

3. **Make the recognition fit the accomplishment.** Be creative! Think of this as the antithesis of the old saw about making the punishment fit the crime. How can you tailor the reward or recognition to uniquely fit the accomplishment. It will mean so much more to the individual or group receiving the credit . . . and reflect much more strongly on you.

4. **Dispense credit and rewards frequently and in a timely fashion.** There's nothing worse than receiving recognition months after the actual achievement. With the passage of time, the initial impact of the accomplishment fades, making any award that much less memorable. Recognize achievements as soon as you can.

5. **Let your team help create the rewards.** Not only will this usually create a stronger, more desirable reward system, it also will enhance your reputation as a leader who cares about how people are treated.

6. **Take blame as readily as you are to dispense credit.** This is a tough one, but you'll earn the respect of employees and superiors alike if you demonstrate your willingness to make the buck stop with you. In most cases, the organization will recognize the real "culprits" and applaud you for your stance. If you have to discipline others, don't shirk from sending a strong message to those at fault, but do it constructively and in private.

The Monkey's Ass

The greater your responsibility, the greater your need to focus on improving your "soft" leadership skills. Remember, the higher the monkey climbs, the more it shows its ass.

"Fighting Joe" Hooker was a man's man and a soldier's soldier. Commanding a Union division during the Civil War, General Hooker won fame as an aggressive and daring commander, one of the few bright spots in a series of reverses, disappointments and outright defeats the North suffered during the early years of the war. Admired by both his men and a public hungry for heroes, Hooker was promoted to commander of the Army of the Potomac in January, 1863.

President Lincoln did so with some reservations, however. In addition to his accomplishments on the field of battle, Hooker had a reputation for heavy drinking, casting fault, quarreling with superiors and peers and political meddling. Lincoln told him point-blank that he was being promoted in spite of, not because of, such asinine comments.

Lincoln might have overlooked all of that if Hooker had demonstrated his trademark success in the field — but he didn't. In fact, his much larger force was soundly beaten by Robert E. Lee's tattered army at the Battle of Chancellorsville. Unable to blame superiors since he was now the supreme commander, Hooker turned on his subordinate generals; one was so disgusted by his commander's poor decisions during the battle that he refused to ever serve under him again.

When Lee invaded the North that summer, Hooker petulantly argued for a counter-invasion of Virginia; Lincoln nixed the idea.

Unable to bring the Confederate army to grips, Hooker complained that Army HQ was undermining his efforts by withholding forces. He impulsively offered his resignation, and Lincoln — who had lost all confidence in "Fighting Joe" — agreed.

THE PETER PARADOX

It's called the Peter Principle, and if you've been in the corporate world for any length of time at all, you've probably seen it firsthand: "Every employee tends to rise to his level of incompetence." Hooker was an excellent division commander, an average corps commander and a downright lousy army commander. We've all seen co-workers who were tremendous at their jobs get "kicked upstairs" only to become a casualty of the new situation. The hit NBC sitcom, *The Office*, is predicated on it; Michael Scott was the company's best salesman, but as a manager he's completely clueless.

The Peter Principle boils down to the simple fact that people fail in positions of greater authority because they think that the skills that got them there will continue to generate success for them. Put another way, what got you where you are won't necessarily keep you there. We should probably call it the Peter *Paradox* instead of the Peter Principle.

That's a tough nut to swallow for those of us who have been taught to keep our heads down and our noses clean, work hard and stick with what works. In that worldview, a promotion was a reward for a job well done. In today's brave new business world, however, it's simply another proving ground. "Do you have what it takes to succeed at this rung of the corporate ladder?" is the implicit question.

We usually think of the Peter Principle in terms of someone like Joe Hooker or Michael Scott, but it's really more subtle and pernicious than that. "Incompetence" is one of those nasty, hurtful words, but if we can take the emotional content out of it for a minute, I think there's a more profound lesson. Incompetence really just means "not having or showing the necessary skills to do something successfully." In the legal realm, it refers to being "not qualified to act in a particular capacity." In medicine, it refers to a body part that is unable to fulfill its function.

Why the semantics lesson? Because incompetence doesn't always mean that you fail spectacularly. It doesn't necessarily mean that you're a moron. It means that the set of skills — the competencies — that you need to be totally successful simply isn't there.

And sometimes those can be a pretty surprising set of skills. Earlier in my career, I was entrusted with the responsibility of running a group of businesses. At the same time, a peer of mine was assigned a similar task. Naturally, we saw each other as (mostly friendly) rivals.

Well, I poured myself into the task, and a year later I was proud of what my group had accomplished. I was also proud that I'd never wasted my boss's time with trivial issues; I simply handled them on my own, checking in with him periodically to keep him informed on our progress.

I also kept an eye on how my rival's group was faring. I noticed that he was meeting much more frequently with senior management, and he took pains to trumpet even minor achievements. "Ah," I thought, "here's a guy who's trying to hide the fact that his group hasn't performed nearly as well as mine by sucking up and blowing smoke. Well, he's not fooling me, and he's sure as hell not going to fool anyone else."

Guess what? He did "fool 'em." The higher-ups raved about how well his group had performed despite all the challenges facing it. Crap! Utter crap! We'd had the same challenges and had still produced better results. Why was he getting all the good press? When he was subsequently promoted ahead of me, I felt disgusted, betrayed . . . and perplexed.

It took me a while to really understand the lesson — the hard lesson — that I'd learned. The solid financial and marketing skills that had put me in that position were all well and good, but I needed a new set of competencies to play at that level: the social and communication skills necessary to impress, persuade and win over my seniors. That's what my rival understood, and what I hadn't.

LEADERSHIP CRISIS: "LISTEN UP, ALL YOU ENTREPRENEURS!"

Relying on "old" skills can be hazardous within an entrepreneurial environment as well. Larry E. Greiner, an associate professor of Organizational Behavior at Havard, wrote a pivotal paper back in 1972 about the five distinct phases that organizations experience as they grow. Each stage is characterized by a dominant management style, which must eventually be changed if the company is to successfully transition to the next phase of growth. In other words, companies need new competencies at each new level, just like individuals do.

Initially, in the "birth stage" of an organization, the emphasis is on creating both a product and a market. Here are some of the most obvious characteristics:

- The company's founders are usually technically or entrepreneurially oriented, and they disdain management activities: their physical and mental energies are absorbed entirely in making and selling a new product.
- Communication among employees is frequent and informal.
- Long hours of work are rewarded by modest salaries and the promise of ownership benefits.
- Control of activities comes from immediate marketplace feedback; the management reacts as customers react.

"All of the foregoing individualistic and creative activities are essential for the company to get off the ground," Greiner wrote. "But therein lies the problem. As the company grows, larger production runs require knowledge about the efficiencies of manufacturing. Increased numbers of employees cannot be managed exclusively through informal communication; new employees are not motivated by an intense dedication to the product or organization. Additional capital must be secured, and new accounting procedures are needed for financial control.

"Thus the founders find themselves burdened with unwanted management responsibilities. So they long for the 'good old days,' still trying to act as they did in the past. At this point, a crisis of leadership occurs. Who is to lead the company out of confusion and solve the managerial problems confronting it? New skills are required, which usually the founders are either unwilling or unable to provide."

From Greiner's research, I think we can extrapolate a lesson that applies equally well to the corporate world and the entrepreneurial arena: the higher you go, the greater the importance of leadership *style* compared to purely technical *competence*.

Time and time again, I've seen the thin line that can separate the effective and ineffective performers. On the face of it, they often appear strikingly similar. Both are usually bright, ambitious and ready to make sacrifices. Both often have outstanding track records. But the ineffective performers ultimately falter because of a flawed interpersonal style, a critical loss of support or an inability to maintain their composure under stress.

Take a look at these top 10 career-killing flaws among executives as cited by the Center for Creative Leadership. Of course, the number one killer is a failure to deliver results, but notice how many of the "softer" management skills make the list:

1. Specific performance problems with the business.
2. Insensitivity to others; abrasive, intimidating or bullying style.
3. Cold, aloof or arrogant.
4. Betrayal of trust.
5. Over-managing – failing to delegate or build a team.
6. Overly ambitious – thinking of next job, playing politics.
7. Failing to staff effectively.
8. Unable to think strategically.
9. Unable to adapt to a boss with different style.
10. Overly dependent on advocate or mentor.

With that in mind, I can't overstate the importance of obtaining an accurate understanding of yourself. "To thine own self be true," wrote Shakespeare, "and it must follow, as the night the day, thou canst not then be false to any man." Play to your leadership strengths without ignoring your weaknesses. Growth isn't a luxury; it's a necessity. It's the competency that you can't live (professionally, at least) without.

Stay aware of how people perceive you. The higher you rise, the more people will be watching you, the higher the standard to which you will be held, and the easier it will be to spot your shortcomings as a leader. Environments change. People change. Businesses change. But the Peter Paradox isn't going away any time soon.

KEYS TO ACTION:

1. **Get an unbiased, third-party assessment of your technical and leadership competencies to form a base.** There are a multitude of formal programs and measurement vehicles from which to choose. Getting a solid understanding of your basic style and technical competencies is important to provide something to push against once new information is obtained.

2. **Schedule a review with your boss . . . and your boss's boss.** In that review talk about the important things: aspirations, values and interests, interpersonal experience, and work history. Forge a clear understanding of their expectations, your perceived strengths and your opportunity areas.

3. **Create a personal advisory board.** Build a stable of people who know you and whose opinions you trust and ask them to provide advice on an ongoing basis.

4. **Get 360-degree feedback.** Your goal should be to try to achieve a balanced, objective feedback loop. Discovering how you are perceived (rightly or wrongly, from your point of view) is the most critical step in understanding where you are starting from and what actions you need to take in both the short and the long term.

5. **Pay attention to long-term trends in feedback.** Remember the old adage, "where there's smoke, there's fire"? It applies to both potential issues and strengths. Look back to determine whether you can identify issues or opportunities that stand out or reoccur. Pay attention to these themes in your personal planning process.

6. **Develop a network beyond your personal advisory board.** Your network should include both those in your immediate work group and those outside it (including customers and suppliers where appropriate). Also include, where possible, those in less senior positions. Often the organization "knows" before the individual does; your goal is to put yourself in a position to know what the organization knows in real time.

7. **Create a personal development plan and track it.**
    Having a personal plan is key. Most people think of
    annual planning exercises as the business "to do" list.
    Make sure that you spend as much time on yourself
    as on the business.

The "You" Brand

You are a brand — build it or lose out to those who are building theirs.

Sarah paced nervously outside the interview room. She desperately wanted this job and everything it offered: new challenges, a terrific work environment and, of course, a sizable salary increase. She mentally rehearsed why she *knew* she was the right candidate: five years at another cutting edge company, experience working side by side with some of the industry's leading lights, repeatedly going above and beyond what was required in her original job description.

Despite those positive self-affirmations, she couldn't keep a cold, thin sliver of doubt from working its way into her thoughts. "Should I have spent more time getting to know people outside the company?" she wondered. "Maybe I should have joined that industry association or that charity that wanted me on their board . . . Would that have really made a difference, though? I mean, my job always came first — I gave it 100 percent of my focus, and it shows in the results I got. Does any of this other stuff really matter?"

Meanwhile, Sarah's competition for the job sat, cool and collected, down the hall. Monique was also bright, committed and a great team player — in fact, her academic credentials were virtually identical to Sarah's. But unlike Sarah, Monique was not only now taking stock of her personal brand. She had begun to consciously build it years before, even hiring a PR person on a small retainer to find opportunities for her to showcase herself: speaking gigs at industry conferences and events, charities that benefited from her expertise, articles for relevant publications. Committed to polishing her brand, she had taken courses in public speaking and even created a personal one-page plan.

The net result of Monique's forethought was that the interview panel had heard of her long before she entered the room. They already had a sense of what she had accomplished and what she stood for. Instead of just a name on a resume page, she came across as a real live person: polished, professional, thoughtful and personable.

The race was over for Sarah before it had even begun.

BRANDING 101

Branding is all around us: the stores we shop in, the cars we aspire to own, the clothes we wear, the wine we sip. Amazing to think it wasn't that long ago that pundits declared the "end of the brand." Apparently they were wrong, since brands are more dominant and pervasive than ever. A good brand can command a premium in whatever market it competes in, so "brand value" is nothing to be scoffed at.

At its core, a brand is really a relationship, the embodiment of the total set of interactions, values and emotions between two parties. It's a sort of emotional contract that implicitly (and sometimes explicitly) tells the customer what they should expect: quality, value, utility, sophistication, uniqueness, etc. The core offerings for which the brand stands for generate a specific set of values or emotions, which become a unique brand "personality."

For example, what do you associate with BMW? Volvo?

Wal-Mart? Neiman Marcus? Apple? Microsoft? I'm willing to bet some very specific — and sometimes very strong — emotions bubble up simply in hearing some of those corporate brands.

When dealing with brands, we tend to think in terms of things, though, rather than people. But consider musicians, comedians, actors and . . . politicians. All of them are keenly aware of their public image; the most successful manufacture a kind of public persona that is designed to elicit specific reactions from their "target market." If I mention, say, Britney Spears, an immediate image no doubt comes to mind for you. While her brand may draw vastly different reactions from teens and boomers, it is nonetheless still a personal brand with a unique set of attributes. If I mention Celine Dion, a completely different set of attributes is conjured up. Each brand, for good or bad, is its own creature.

Whether you know it or not, you too have a personal brand. We sometimes call it by other names like reputation, standing, personality, character. Regardless of the term we use, the point here is that others already see you as a unique set of attributes and values. So the real question becomes: do you know what your brand is? Are you maximizing its value?

YOU ARE A PRODUCT

Branding yourself is really no different than branding a company, product or service. Unfortunately, that means that although you may influence it, in the final analysis it's all about how others see you. They own the perception and thus create the brand. Your task is to help favorably shape that perception.

Strong brands share three main characteristics:

1. *Relevance:* A brand must be connected to a specific individual or group.
2. *Differentiation:* The brand must be perceived as distinctive in some way.
3. *Consistency:* The values, relevance and differentiation that are embedded in the brand must be regularly demonstrated and communicated to the target audience.

Let's talk about relevance first. The key to creating relevance is seeing your personal brand from the *outside-in*. In order to understand how to impact others, you must first learn to understand their world, their needs and their opinions. Relevance comes from delivering solutions and actions that are valued from others' perspectives . . . not necessarily yours.

"Differentiate or die!" is a mainstay of corporate branding strategy. A strong personal brand is equally unique. There is only one Richard Branson, Donald Trump or Madonna — and only one you. Why should clients or customers choose you instead of one of your competitors? What is special and authentic about you?

Differentiation, by its very nature, entails risk. It is the path less traveled, and there is no denying that there is often safety in numbers. There's also mediocrity and ultimately fewer rewards. Standing out means taking a stand. For that very reason, personal brand differentiation must be solidly rooted in your fundamental value system.

The final ingredient for a strong brand is consistency. Your personal brand must deliver the same message, through every "channel," every time. You can't stand for ethics and integrity if even one example contradicts that image — ask any televangelist busted for tax fraud, embezzlement or adultery. Only repetition will build trust in your brand, the same way that a scientific theory must deliver the same set of results each time an experiment is conducted in order to be accepted as fact. Fail to deliver with consistency and your personal brand will likely end up the opposite of what you intended.

KEYS TO ACTION:

1. **Define your brand "essence" from the inside-out.** The process starts with a journey of self-discovery. The first step is to very clearly identify your core values. You can use one of a myriad of assessment tools freely available to better understand the "inner" you. You may even have had the luxury of personal development exercises through your workplace — if so, you're ahead of the game. Whatever path you choose, the goal is to write down a short list of values that are absolutely core to the way you live your life. These are non-negotiable and form the core of your personal "essence."

2. **Build a composite "sketch" of yourself from the outside-in.** This is tougher because it relies on obtaining an accurate view of the commonly held perceptions about you from your external stakeholders. (If possible, use a third party to discover

them, as your chances of getting reliable data are much higher than if you do it yourself.) Use the same set of variables that you used to build your own perception about your defined core values. It is very important to see whether the outside view matches the inner assessment. It is also important to determine whether there are inherent differences across the various stakeholders. Do your coworkers see you differently than your friends?

3. **Identify your target market and its needs.** If your desire is to build a strong personal brand within the work environment, you must very clearly identify your target market. Is it your superiors? Your employees and coworkers? A broader set of the business community? Remember, since the value of your brand ultimately depends on your target market's perception of it, you need a deep understanding of its needs and how you best can service those needs.

4. **Identify your unique brand benefit.** Forrest Gump spent a lot of time looking for his "special purpose." The brand benefit is *your* special purpose, the *one thing* you do best that addresses your target group's issues or needs. Head and Shoulders cleans hair, helps repair split ends and conditions, but the real brand benefit is that it fights dandruff. To be valued, there must be a meeting of the minds between your brand

promise and the needs of your target group — Head and Shoulders' promise doesn't mean that much to someone who doesn't have a dandruff problem. The key is understanding what your unique brand benefit is and then matching it to the people who need it most.

5. **Plan your action, then action your plan.** One of the benefits of the Plan on a Page process outlined earlier in the book is that the same principles can be applied to your personal brand. Create a plan to present your brand to the market.

Unlearning Your Golf Swing

Discarding old habits and ideas is the real key to remaining effective and relevant.

The Royal Navy in the 19th century was the pride of Great Britain. From sleek frigates to powerful three-decker ships of the line, the expertly crewed British vessels struck fear in their opponents, especially after Admiral Nelson decimated a larger Franco-Spanish fleet at the Battle of the Trafalgar. The victory definitively ended any plans Napoleon had to invade England and helped plant the seeds of his eventual defeat.

With the advent of the Age of Steam, however, technology threatened the Royal Navy's supremacy far more than any enemy fleet ever did. Elderly commanders often resented or failed to understand the steam-powered engines fitted onto their ships, preferring to rely on the same tried and true techniques they had learned as midshipmen in the navy of their youth.

One such captain, entering a harbor under both sail and steam, gave orders to strike the sails and lower anchor. To his amazement, the ship continued toward shore, snapping the anchor cable. Just before running aground, a junior officer reminded the captain that he had failed to order the engines stopped.

"Bless me," the grizzled veteran replied, "I forgot we *had* engines."

THE QUEST FOR THE PERFECT GOLF SWING

I suck at golf.

That's a hard thing for me to admit, but the fact is that for every booming, 280-yard, straight-as-an-arrow drive, I probably shank three drives into the rough or chop them short. Years of practice haven't really fixed the problem, and all too often one of my golf outings becomes, in the words of Mark Twain, "a good walk spoiled."

I know I'm not alone. Talk to any golfer (irrespective of their ability) and — if they're being honest — they'll admit that they dream endlessly about perfecting their golf swing. So why do so few of us reach that lofty goal? And why do so many of us try to heed the well-meaning advice of our fellow golfers ("If I were you, I'd strengthen my grip and put more weight on my back foot coming through the ball."), only to send a drive screaming like a cruise missile right into the nearest bird's nest?

Believe me, I've spent a lot of time pondering the problem. And I finally heard the advice that crystallized the dilemma: before you can learn the perfect swing, you have to unlearn all the bad habits that make your swing imperfect.

OBSOLETE AT 30

My wife, who heads a large marketing department for a large national retailer, recently emailed me an article written by a well-known media pundit. The article focused on coming trends within the industry and the impact of new technologies. It was bleeding edge stuff (even to someone like me who tries to keep relatively current), and it took me several reads to get the gist of it. Even then, a few of the more technical aspects were lost on me. "Does this make you feel like a dinosaur, too?" my wife asked me. Somewhat reluctantly, I had to admit . . . yes.

What really struck me out of the episode is that here we were, two very senior and experienced marketing types, leaders in our field — and this article made us feel like college freshmen again! The topics the article covered hadn't even existed two years ago. That's how fast the industry is changing, and the pace of that change is accelerating.

Want an even more disturbing example? Just the other day I was speaking to a young man responsible for creating one of the hottest marketing companies of the last decade, a company at the forefront of developing new mobile content and advertising. He told me that *he* too felt like a dinosaur . . . at age 30! He said he was having trouble keeping up with the 20-somethings he was hiring. Not only that, he said he even noticed what almost seemed like a generation gap between the employees in their mid-20s and those in their early 20s! Wondering if change is really occurring that quickly? Believe it.

Change is threatening to most of us because it questions, even invalidates, the lessons we've learned the hard way and the skills we've acquired through the sweat of our brow. Once advertising was confined to print. Then radio came along. Then television. Then the Internet, and mobile phones, and PDAs . . . and who knows what's next? (I often say that the next thing will be to implant a chip in each of us capable of performing those tasks; after that, genetic programming will become a reality.) The generation that cut its teeth on the principles of radio advertising had to unlearn what worked in the older medium and acquire a completely different set of skills to thrive in the age of television. Failure to do so meant assured obsolescence.

We're all in the same situation, regardless of industry. Here are just a few examples of areas that demand you regularly unlearn what worked last year so you can master what will work *next* year:

- Rapidly changing target markets filled with more informed (and demanding) customers.
- Employees who put their needs and goals ahead of the company's.
- Communication technology that allows you to stay in touch with customers, vendors and others.
- Branding.
- Geographic reach that allows you to effectively market in a global economy.

FIVE HUNDRED SWINGS

Unlearning is counterintuitive. A new golf swing feels unnatural and abnormal, and it's easy to fall back into old habits. That's why so many companies prefer to hire untrained people — it's ultimately easier to train them from scratch instead of trying to first break them of previously learned habits.

Experts say that changing the muscle memory involved in a golf swing requires hitting it correctly a whopping 500 times in succession. Five hundred times! And you have to think, feel and act against the old swing, each and every time, until the new swing becomes habit.

Is all this hassle really worth it? Consider the words of London Business School professor Charles Handy: "If change is, as I have argued, only another word for learning, the theories of learning will also be the theories of changing. Those who are always learning are those who can ride the waves of change and who see a changing world as full of opportunities rather than damage. They are the ones most likely to be the survivors in a time of discontinuity."

Sure enough, a recent study confirms that CEOs and senior leaders who become adept at unlearning old skills and continually learning new ones possess significant advantages over those who remain rooted in their old ways. These executives, who regularly question, listen and learn from others on a variety of very disparate subjects, also:

- On average live longer (and remain active longer) than their peers.
- Are more effective leaders, able to formulate better solutions to challenges because of their broader knowledge base.
- Report feeling more fulfilled, with higher levels of "contentment."
- Are more optimistic, seeing the glass as "half full" rather than "half empty."
- Inspire those around them.
- Are more effective change agents.
- Are more likely to survive change themselves.

A few years ago, the process of continual unlearning and relearning was optional. Now it's an imperative for anyone who wants to keep up their intellectual relevance in a rapidly changing world. The choice is yours: adapt and survive or, like that old British naval captain, ignore the future and run aground.

KEYS TO ACTION:

1. **Recognize the need to unlearn.** This can be a humbling step — but the thought that you may be a dinosaur is even more disturbing. If you find yourself using the same stories over and over to illustrate a point, if people no longer ask your advice in an area in which you were once regarded as an expert, if you stubbornly cling to tried-and-true habits simply because "that's the way we've always done things," then it's probably time to start unlearning.

2. **You need to know how to change, not why.** There are plenty of authors, therapists and advice gurus out there who will focus on why you're in the position you're in. Screw that — it doesn't matter *why* you ended up teetering on the edge of obsolescence, only *how* you re-establish relevance. If your golf swing sucks, it sucks. What are you going to do about it?

3. **Get qualified help.** You can't unlearn alone; just as a golfer needs a seasoned golf pro to show him the flaws in his swing, you need experts to help you understand how old habits and antiquated methods of operation are hindering your success. The quality of the instruction you receive has a direct bearing on the result, so remember: just because someone is willing to provide advice doesn't mean they know what they're talking about. Take the time to

understand the real need and pre-qualify the resources and advisors you engage — then listen to them.

4. **Eliminate old habits.** Practice, practice, practice. It's hard work, often unfulfilling work, but there's no other way to unlearn.

5. **Replace old habits with new ones.** Recognizing the need to unlearn involves thinking and insight. Eliminating old habits involves feeling and motivation. Replacing the old with something new requires dedication and repetition. You must force yourself to think, feel and act against your former instincts until the new habit feels as natural as the old one once did.

The Doomsday Question
Your business doesn't need you as much as you think it does. Working "in" your business can be detrimental to its health ... and yours.

How's this for a "what if" scenario: right in the middle of prime time, every television broadcast is interrupted, replaced by a graphic of the Presidential seal. A moment later, you see the President himself, seated behind that big desk in the Oval Office. He looks like he's aged ten years overnight.

"Ladies and gentlemen," he begins somberly. "I come before you this evening as the bearer of grave news. A little over three months ago, NASA's long-range scanners detected an immense asteroid on a collision course with Earth. To prevent widespread panic, this news was kept under the tightest of security, although it was shared with the governments of the world's developed countries.

"For the past three months, these nations have, in an unprecedented display of global co-operation, undertaken several attempts to destroy or deflect this threat. It is with the heaviest of hearts, however, that I must report to you that all our efforts have proved unsuccessful. Our scientists calculate that the asteroid will strike the Pacific Ocean tomorrow at approximately 12:25 PM GMT.

"Given its size, the immediate and residual damage will effectively destroy all life on this planet. We have come to a point that none of us believed possible: the end of mankind. In the face of this impending cataclysm, I encourage all of you to prepare yourselves in whatever way you deem most appropriate. Good night, good luck and may God have mercy on us all."

TAKING A BREAK

A colleague of mine told the above story at a retreat for owners and managers of small and medium-sized business enterprises (SMEs). He paused for a moment, then looked directly at the audience.

"After hearing this, I'd like those folks to raise their hands whose first thought was 'I need to get back to the office.'" To no one's surprise, every hand in the room stayed down. "Then tell me," my friend said, "would it really take doomsday for you to take a real break from your business?"

It's a question well worth pondering. Whether you own a business or are trying to get ahead in a major corporation, the fact is that today's professional culture implicitly discourages time off. Even if you're not in the office, there's an unspoken assumption that you'll be checking email and voicemail. That's what your BlackBerry is for, after all . . . isn't it?

Not that it's all a matter of peer pressure, either. Much of our inability to distance ourselves from our business is self-imposed. I can hear some of you now: "Sure, my wife and kids have been nagging me for years to slow down and smell the roses, but if I took time away from the business, it would suffer. My family and friends don't understand how critical it is for me to be in front of my customers and to be seen to be working alongside my employees. They need me!"

They need you, all right — they need you to back off. And I'm not talking just about more vacation time here, either.

NO MORE TRAINING WHEELS

We've all heard the advice that you've got to work *on*, not *in* your business. I've heard very few people really dispute it — and seen very few people actually follow it. The reality is that most of us got to where we are professionally by rolling up our sleeves and doing what needed to be done. Entrepreneurs are especially notorious for adopting a hands-on approach to all aspects of their enterprises. The company is their brainchild, their baby, and it needs them day and night.

And they're right — for a while. But like children, companies grow up. The baby that needed Momma to do everything for him eventually wants to take the training wheels off the bike and ride it himself. No matter how much you want to, you can't run behind the bike holding it up forever; at some point you have to let go.

That letting go is a good thing. I know you feel deeply attached to your business, that you view it with a complicated mix of emotions: part responsibility, part pride of ownership and part fear that the business will slide if you're not involved in every detail. You're not alone. I think virtually every businessperson feels those same emotions. The truly great ones, however, understand when it's time to let go.

The hard truth is that we like "getting dirty" in our business. It makes us feel important and wanted... to be the problem-solver everyone turns to. It makes us feel needed and part of the team. It makes us feel busy. Unfortunately, it also makes us ineffective. How often have you returned home after a long day at the office feeling like you haven't accomplished anything of any substance? Sure, you helped Mary deal with a shipping problem, and Fred resolve a personal issue with another employee, and surfed the web for a couple of hours to give your marketing guys some ideas for the next big promotion . . . but at the end of the day, was this really the best use of your time?

Unintentionally, we've taught our co-workers to come to us with their problems, questions and issues, instead of letting them handle things themselves. In its most basic form, empowerment is about letting go so that responsibility for a task lies with the person closest to the issue, the person who usually has the best understanding of what's required. Historian Stephen Ambrose attributed the success of the American army during the Normandy invasion to the fact that, while hidebound and bureaucratic in the barracks, it became supremely flexible on the battlefield, empowering even junior officers and NCOs to overcome the obstacles in front of them instead of referring everything back up the chain of command. Businesses need to have that same versatility.

I remember a customer service nightmare I experienced at a major retail chain last year. Instead of dealing with my relatively simple issue, the employee I was talking to told me, "I'm going to have to check with my manager." Fifteen minutes later, I was still standing there, doing a slow burn. The manager, I assume, was on break or engaged in some other task. By the time my issue was finally resolved, I'd resolved never to shop there again. Who's at fault for that dissatisfaction, the employee or the manager? In my view, it's the manager because he hadn't allowed or taught his employee how to act independently.

SUPPORTING ROLE

Working *on* your business requires that you play a role very different than you've been accustomed to. It means a move from "being on the field" to supporting those who are. That can be tough — let's face it, wouldn't we all rather play than coach?

But the benefits of working *on*, rather than *in*, are immediate and significant. Freed from the compulsion to be the first one in the office and the last one out every day, you'll likely feel more rested, recharged and creative. Because you'll be out and about more, you'll be able to expand your network. You'll also begin seeing your business as others do, from the outside-in. As a result, you'll be able to produce significant change in the company for the better, positioning it to respond to customers' real needs and desires. And last — but certainly not least — you'll see an improvement in the quality of your personal and family life.

A corollary to the principle of working on your business is the necessity to take time away from it, even in non-vacation situations. While working with the Stephen Covey group one year, I noted an effective, if counterintuitive technique for daily planning. Most days I've spent with trainers feature scheduled breaks every two hours or so. On this day, however, we were strongly encouraged to break on the 50-minute mark of every hour for 10 minutes. That's a 10-minute break each hour!

We all scoffed at the suggestion, but I have to admit that in hindsight it was the most effective day I've ever spent in a group. After the meeting, people felt energized rather than worn out. I've since used the practice in my business with the same result, and I'm certain you'll benefit from it as well. Taking short, frequent breaks will refresh you and boost your creativity. That in turn means better ideas and increased productivity — and that's a recipe for good business.

KEYS TO ACTION:

1. **Create a "top three" process.** Write down the three items that, if completed during this day/week/month, would represent a significant accomplishment. Then make their completion your top priority, gauging every activity by its impact on your ability to get the top three completed. I've even used this in lieu of the dreaded annual employee review, jointly identifying at the beginning of the year the three things that, if successfully accomplished during the next 12 months, would mean a job performance home run.

2. **Build "you" time into your calendar.** Regularly plan blocks of time for planning, catching up, doing some writing, preparing a proposal or even catching a few winks. Be ruthless about keeping this personal time personal and you'll be surprised at how much more effective you'll become.

3. **Create a plan and stick to it.** It's said that 85 percent or so of small businesses have no plan at all. That's a recipe for disaster. Having a plan helps ensure that activity is directed and focused. With fewer chances to become side-tracked, work usually becomes more productive.

4. **Combine your business and personal calendar.** This runs counter to our penchant to compartmentalize our professional and home lives, but I've found it to be very effective. Actually listing family activities on

your calendar makes them more visible, elevating their relative importance and more easily allowing you to plan around them.

6. **Delegate.** The old adage of teaching your people how to fish instead of giving them a fish is the operative philosophy here. In the short term, it's always quicker to do the work yourself, but in the long run delegating certain functions will free you up for more important activities and improve workplace morale.

7. **Appoint a personal "advisory board."** Find a few trusted advisors or family members to help monitor your work-life balance and hold you accountable. We don't always notice when that balance gets out of whack, so an outside-in perspective in this area (as in so many others) can be very useful.

Appendix A:
Strategy Development Workbook

"SWOT" DEVELPOPMENT

The purpose of developing a "SWOT" is to accurately assess the current situation for a company, brand, product or service. When complete, it provides an accurate snapshot of where it stands today from an internal and a market perspective. Ideally, a "SWOT" would be completed first on an individual (personal) basis followed by a group discussion. An ideal process would also provide outside-in (i.e. external feedback) to ensure that the internal view is consistent with that of your external stakeholders. Examples of external stakeholders would be customers, shareholders, suppliers etc.

A "SWOT" is an encapsulation of what is known about the current situation from both a quantitative and a qualitative standpoint. Wherever possible, fact is used to support the conclusions within a SWOT. SWOT statements are intended to represent true INSIGHT about your current situation drawn from these facts, not merely facts themselves.

Strengths and weaknesses (S&W of the SWOT) are internal

elements. They relate to the company, brand, product or service that is the focus of the strategic exercise. Opportunities and Threats (O&T of the SWOT) are external elements. Together they are intended to form a 360-degree view of the current situation.

<u>Strengths</u>: **List those areas you consider to be your key leverage areas. These are things you do particularly well or have at your command to use to advantage in the market.**

(Here are some questions to prime the pump.)

- What is the single most important thing that your company offers to its customers?
- Think about how you deliver your "product" to your customers. What are the key strengths of that delivery?
- Are your employees a key source of strength?
- Do you have strategic relationships that yield strength?
- Have your strengths changed over time? What has changed? Why?
- What would your customers say are your key strengths? Do you think that list would change if you asked a number of them, or would they stay consistent across the group?
- What key things got you to where you are today?
- What learning have you had over the past years that would support your list of strengths? Have you any quantitative data?
- Who do you consider to be your primary target group? What would they say your strengths to be? What would your competition say?

- Think across all of your activities running down your financials. Are there areas in which you have excelled? Why?

<u>Strengths</u>:

<u>Weaknesses</u>: (Generally the reverse of strengths.) List those areas you consider to be your Achilles heel(s). These are areas that you feel are areas for improvement. Some will be more critical than others. Again, from an overall standpoint, it is better to start this process individually, then move to group discussion. Quantitative support and outside-in perspective is also a plus.

Again, some questions to kick-start the process . . .

- Are there particular areas of performance in which you have noted chronic issues?
- Have you any quantitative support for these issues?
- What have customers highlighted as specific issues in the past? Are any of these chronic?
- What have employees cited as issues?
- Do you have any concerns over responsiveness to market conditions or customer issues?
- Do your customers find your activity in-market to be relevant and beneficial?
- Have you issues with churn or retention?
- Are there particular areas that you come up short relative to your competition? Are these well known?
- Are there any barriers to addressing any or all of these weaknesses?
- Think about companies in other industries with issues you've noted. Do you share any of these issues?
- What would you least be prepared to tackle as a new initiative? Why? What skill do you lack?

Weaknesses:

<u>Opportunities</u>: We now turn to those areas we consider to be underleveraged but possible in improving our current position. They can be remarkable or merely invigorating. Opportunities represent those items that provide for acceleration of performance or a breakthrough to a different level. They can be sponsored by a twist of an internal program or access to a here-to-fore underleveraged external trend or situation.

Some questions:

- Are there potential new targets for your service?
- Which customer segments are growing the fastest and, if accessed, could provide accelerated growth?
- Are there ideas that people in your organization have had that are sitting on the shelf? Were they ahead of their time? Is the time now right to re-explore them?
- Are there other industries or businesses that could provide a "learning laboratory" for your business? Other geographies?
- Are there things that you are doing now as an organization that with a little push or investment could yield much stronger results?
- If you could wave a magic wand and you had all the resources in the world, are there areas that you would pursue? Which ones?
- Can you steal any great ideas from anywhere else and twist them so they become your own?
- Can you think of other ways to use your existing services or products that could open up new revenue sources?

- Have you asked your customers and other partners what they would like to see? Have they offered ideas in the past? Are there any that make sense?
- Could you reallocate some of your existing resources to generate higher return?
- Are there ways to partner with others or partner differently that offer a new set of opportunities?

<u>Opportunities</u>:

Threats: Create a list of those things that could create issues for your forward progression (either your existing or contemplated plan). Consider things like trends that could go awry, new competition, emerging technology, regulations, commodity or currency spikes.

Some questions:

- Would your customers or other external stakeholders see things in the way you are doing business or on the horizon that could spell trouble?
- If you asked a third party to comment on the threats facing your business, what would their answer be?
- Are there any market conditions that warrant special attention given their potential impact. Growth prospects? Regulatory? Killer Technologies? Competition?
- Do other companies have a preferred competitive position? Are they making up ground on our leadership position? How?
- Do we have the resources, including real knowledge of being able to compete in the broader arena for the longer term?
- Is there a strong barrier to entry for others outside of our market? If we were wildly successful with a new plan, who would enter and could we remain successful?
- Do you have processes in place to stay ahead?
- Could there be a fundamental change in the market (i.e. consolidation) that could change the competitive balance?
- What would be the worst thing you could imagine

that could happen that would put your business in jeopardy?

<u>Threats</u>:

"FROM – TO" Strategy Statement

Looking back over your SWOT, create one or two sentences that summarize your insight about your current situation. This statement is the bedrock upon which you will build your future but also the inflection point from which you will transform. It represents the jumping off point to your new direction. It is the "FROM" portion of a strategic summary statement that includes both a "From" and a "To".

The "FROM" Statement (example):

Kraft Dinner is a Canadian brand icon. It has established deep, strong personal ties with its consumers, but faces diminishing growth prospects in a maturing demographic and category. Kraft Dinner also faces short-term margin pressure, a result of escalating commodity prices and limited upward pricing flexibility.

From: Dry Mac 'N Cheese "Youth" pasta...

SWOT "FROM" Summary: Describe your current situation in two sentences or less as a distillation of your SWOT analyses.

The "TO" Statement

If the "From" Statement is where you are, the next exercise is intended to help define where you need to go over the next few years.

Start with a review of the Strengths and Opportunities identified through your SWOT analysis. This should provide ample fodder for development of where you need to go. The reason to start with the review of these two areas is that it starts with possibilities and areas which provide leverage. Don't be concerned that you don't have the capability to get there as you stand now. Part of the next step will determine what you need to bring with you from your past, what you need to drop or change and what new capabilities you need to develop.

The "TO" Statement (example):

Kraft Dinner will leverage its strong brand icon status and expand its business to encompass all forms of consumer preparation (dry, frozen and refrigerated). It will build a strengthened presence in portion controlled products for improved margin as well as an expanded line of products in growing segments beyond macaroni and cheese to capture new pasta trends and consumption habits.

To: Convenient "Youth" food available in all forms of preparation.

SWOT "TO" Summary Statement: In two sentences or less, describe where you need to take your business over the next few years to remain successful.

Key Issues/Gaps:

The key issues/gaps section of a strategic planning exercise provides a summary of those challenges requiring resolution and action over the timeframe. These issues must be generated within the context of your "TO" statement. What are things you need to accomplish or overcome in order to meet your stated objectives and end point?

Key issues are not just issues or problems. A key issue could also be the challenge in leveraging a strength and translating that into a return for the business. The operative word is KEY. All businesses face innumerable challenges. The challenge for the strategic planning exercise is to focus down on those which, if resolved or dealt with successfully, will drive positive momentum and return. The fewer the number, the more focused the action through the organization.

Key Issues Summary: List your top three key issues. Remember that key issues can be both weaknesses and strengths.

1)

2)

3)

At this point in our exercise, you should be able to communicate very succinctly, where you are coming from, where you are going and what you need to do to get there. In our Kraft Dinner example it could read as follows:

Kraft Dinner is a Canadian brand icon facing growth and margin challenges because of maturing category dynamics, rising commodity costs and a low inflation environment. We must expand its presence into new growing segments (refrigerated, frozen and dry) better aligned with consumer consumption trends. In order to accomplish this we must successfully address three key issues:

1. **Lack of expertise and business system in refrigerated and frozen distribution channels.**

2. **Weak proven product development funnel.**

3. **Ability to carry brand into "higher end" consumer trends and consumption occasions.**

Key Thrusts/Strategies

Once the key issues have been identified, the next step is to identify the key thrusts or strategies that will be required to accomplish your business objectives. These should be limited to five key thrusts. Some suggestions in terms of core thrusts.

1) New areas of growth.
2) Improvement in production or channel capability.
3) People. Building new competencies.
4) Customers. Refining current ones, building new ones.
5) Core process improvements.
6) External development (i.e. acquisitions or divestiture).
7) Cost reduction.

KEY THRUSTS/SRATEGIES: Thinking about your Strategic Assessment and Key Issues Summary, identify up to 5 key thrusts which will require focus over the timeframe to achieve success.

1)

2)

3)

4)

5)

Actions, Timing and Responsibility

In this section, you must identify the specific actions or projects that will be required to address each of the strategic thrusts. Timing and overall responsibility for the project must also be identified. It is important at this stage that there be no joint accountability for a project. Only one name must accompany each project. It must be owned by only one person. Again, core projects only are to be included in each list.

List those projects, timing and key accountability required to progress each key thrust.

1) Build top line growth.

-
-
-

2) Expand production/channel capability into...

-
-
-

3) Build human resource base and competency.

-
-
-

4) Strengthen and expand customer base.

-

-

-

5) Improve core business processes.

-

-

-

Establishing Key Performance Indicators (KPIs)

We've now completed a situation assessment (your SWOT); established a strategic summary statement (the From – To); identified the key challenges to be overcome and the key thrusts and action items, including timing and responsibility. We now need to determine those things that we wish to measure in order to determine organizational progress and accountability over the timeframe.

This is the KPI list. Again, it should be focused. Some examples:

- Cash flow
- Revenue (growth, size)
- Margin
- EBITDA
- Service levels
- Cost/Productivity
- People

IDENTIFY YOUR KPI LIST (up to but not exceeding 5):

1)

2)

3)

4)

5)

Congratulations, you've just completed the key elements of your strategic plan! This plan can be easily formatted to fit onto one page for easy reference as per the attached sample.

Appendix B:
Plan On A Page Template

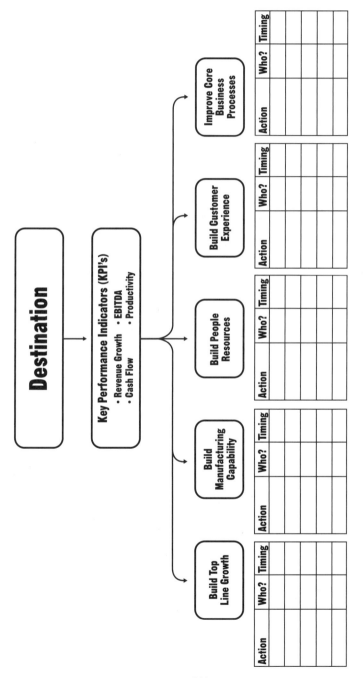

Appendix C:
Additional Resources

- *Build Your Customer Strategy* by James G. Barnes (John Wiley and Sons, 2006).

- *The Six Fundamentals of Success* by Stuart R. Levine (Doubleday, 2004).

- *You're in Charge: Now What?* by Thomas J. Neff & James M. Citrin (Three Rivers Press (2005).

- *Wikinomics* by Don Tapscott & Anthony D. Williams (Penguin, 2007).

- *Brain Tattoos* by Karen Post (Amacom, 2005).

- *CEO Tools* by Kraig Kramers (Gandy Dancer Press, 2002).

- *The Streetsmart Marketer*, 2006   Michael Hepworth, Manor House Publishing

- *Big Business Marketing for Small Business Budgets* by Jeanette Maw McMurtry (McGraw-Hill, 2003).

- *Good to Great* by Jim Collins (Harper Collins, 2001).

- *The Prince* by Niccolo Machiavelli (multiple publishers).

- *Get Smarter* by Seymour Schulich (Key Porter Books, 2007).

- *Creating Competitive Advantage* by Jaynie L. Smith (Doubleday, 2006).

- *Taking Charge: Lessons in Leadership* by Jim Kouzes, Jim Tunney and Warren G. Bennis (Insight Publishing and Saga Worldwide, Inc., 2003).

- *Companies Are People, Too* by Sandra Fekete with LeeAnna Keith (John Wiley and Sons, 2003).

- *Purple Cow* by Seth Godin (Penguin Group, 2003).

- *Ultimate Leadership* by John C. Maxwell (Thomas Nelson, 2001).

- *Please Understand Me II* by David Keirsey (Prometheus Nemesis Book Company, 1998).

- *What Got You Here Won't Get You There* by Marshall Goldsmith with Mark Reiter (Hyperion, 2007).

- www.vistage.com

- www.12manage.com

- www.wikipedia.org.